MYTHS AND LEGENDS
OF THE GARDEN

Roman fresco of Flora, goddess of flowers and spring

MYTHS AND LEGENDS
OF THE GARDEN

John and Rosemary Hemphill

Hodder & Stoughton

A Hodder & Stoughton Book

Published in Australia and New Zealand in 1997
by Hodder Headline Australia Pty Limited,
(A member of the Hodder Headline Group)
10–16 South Street, Rydalmere NSW 2116

Published by arrangement with Lansdowne Publishing Pty Ltd, Sydney

National Library of Australia Cataloguing-in-Publication data

Hemphill, John.
Myths and Legends of the garden.

ISBN 0 7336 0480 3.

1. Plants - Mythology. 2. Fruit - Mythology.
I. Hemphill, Rosemary. II. Title.

398.242

Front cover: *A Tribute to Bacchus*, Jean-Baptists Robie, 1821–1910

Printed in China

To Diana

ABOUT THE AUTHORS

WITH OVER FORTY YEARS experience in herb cultivation and usage, John and Rosemary Hemphill are leading authorities on herbs and their history and have lectured extensively on the subject. Rosemary's first book *Fragrance and Flavour* was awarded a bronze medal at Frankfurt in 1960 and together, John and Rosemary have written several highly acclaimed books including *Hemphill's Book of Herbs, Hemphill's Herbs their cultivation and usage* and *Hemphill's Herbs for Health.*

The romance and mystique surrounding plants has always held Rosemary's respect and her love for the subject is revealed in the gentle style she has adopted in her interpretation of the myths and legends.

CONTENTS

Left: A Tribute to Bacchus, JEAN-BAPTISTE ROBIE, 1821 – 1910

INTRODUCTION

MYTHS AND LEGENDS take us into a wondrous world of imagination, fantasy and dreams. They are part of the culture of every tribe or civilization, and it is surprising to discover how similar to each other are the characters, stories and folklore of peoples quite distant from one another in both time and place.

Among the early peoples, the first legends were explanations of the creation of the world. One Greek myth narrates that in the beginning there was a conglomeration of earth, sea and air, all mixed up together and spinning in space, and given the name Chaos. The Creator separated from Chaos the earth, the sea, the skies, the air, and heaven. Heavenly seeds from Chaos lay dormant in the earth, and humankind was moulded from these into the image of God, the Creator.

This legend's portrayal of the earth's beginning coincides with the Bible's Genesis, Chapter 1, which gives a similar description of Creation:

> *In the beginning God created the heaven and the earth. And the earth was without form, and void; and darkness was upon the face of the deep. And the Spirit of God moved upon the face of the waters. And God said, Let there be light: and there was light.*

(GENESIS 2 V. 7)

The myths and legends of most cultures have a similar basis: they explain the creation of the world and its creatures and plants in terms that are credible to the people of that particular culture. The Australian Aborigines' culture is based on their belief in the Dreamtime, from which springs a huge range of legends explaining their surroundings. The folklore of ancient Egypt had similar themes to other civilizations, but each myth holds a fascinating twist that expresses a particular era of the great Pharaohs, while China's vast history through the dynasties is embellished with tales of the gods the people worshipped.

Many cultures and civilizations adapted the myths and legends of others to suit their own unique worlds. Many Greek deities were derived from earlier Babylonian and Egyptian gods and goddesses. The Romans adopted Greek myths, incorporating them into their own, but Latinizing some of the Greek names. Christian legends, like the story of Joseph of Arimathea and the Glastonbury Thorn, are nearer in time to the present day and quite well authenticated; Arthurian legends, although even closer to our time, are thought to be partly in the realm of myth, but are founded on the life of an outstanding leader and hero of the 6th century A.D.

Since the beginning of recorded history, humankind of all civilizations has created immortal or "other-world" beings. These mythical entities were created to mirror life on earth and help explain the mysteries of nature and the universe — birth, love, life, and death. As a first form of religion, myths reveal to us the psychology of primitive peoples and the very nature of human beings.

Numerous gods and goddesses were connected with vegetation, as early civilizations relied heavily on plant life and agriculture for their food. The early peoples worshipped the deities who made their crops prosper and their orchards blossom. Magical plants with uncanny effects feature in myths and legends from the earliest days of recorded history, and were used in many cultures in the rituals and practices of magicians, witches, and medicine men.

It is widely believed that humans are united with the earth, and that our affinity with plant life is in our genes. The fascinating myths and legends in this book have been specially selected to reflect the close bond between humankind and the earth's wonderfully abundant array of herbs, flowers, fruit, and trees.

ANCIENT
GREEK AND ROMAN

The myths of the ancient Greeks and Romans have become a valuable part of art and literature; they also give us an idea of the culture and lifestyle of these ancient peoples. The Romans adopted Greek myths, but Latinized some of the deities' names. They also created their own myths. The last two stories in this chapter, the first about Flora, the goddess of flowers and spring, the other about Pomona and Vertumnus are good examples of Roman mythology.

In mythology, the gods and goddesses of Greece lived forever. They moved among the stars and had their home on the summit of Mount Olympus, a tall mountain in the north of Greece. They entered their celestial dwelling through a gate of clouds, and there feasted on nectar and ambrosia while listening to the god Apollo's golden lyre. Reigning over all was Zeus (Jupiter), the King, and Hera (Juno), his Queen. Hera was selfish and jealous of Zeus, and often made the lives of others miserable. However, the immortals did as they pleased, descending to earth frequently to interact with mortals, and with nymphs, satyrs, centaurs and other magical beings. The gods and goddesses of Mount Olympus were amorous; they often fell in love with one another, and sometimes with nymphs and mortals. The romances of these encounters, which frequently featured plant life, have been recounted again and again. They gave substance and boundaries to the unknown, for the people of ancient Greece believed all their joys and sorrows came from the whims and blessing of their deities.

GODS AND GODDESSES
OF
ANCIENT GREECE AND ANCIENT ROME

GREEK NAME	ROMAN NAME
APHRODITE	VENUS
ARES	MAR
ARTEMIS	DIANA
ATHENA (Sometimes PALLAS ATHENA)	MINERVA
DIONYSUS	BACCHUS
DEMETER	CERES
EOS	AURORA
EROS	CUPID
HADES, AIDES	PLUTO
HEPHAESTUS	VULCAN
HERA	JUNO
HERMES	MERCURY
POSEIDON	NEPTUNE
PERSEPHONE	PROSERPINA
ZEUS	JUPITER, JOVE

ACHILLES AND YARROW
(Achillea millefolium)

IN ANCIENT times, in Greece, there lived a water nymph by the name of Thetis. Thetis was so beautiful that Zeus (Jupiter), the father of gods and men, desired her for his wife. But then he learned of a prophecy which told that Thetis would bear a son who would be greater than his father. Zeus withdrew his suit and decreed that Thetis should be the wife of a mortal. Thetis married King Peleus of the Myrmidons in Thessaly and they had a son, Achilles.

It had been prophesied that Achilles would be a great warrior, but that he would die in battle. In an attempt to protect her son, Thetis dipped the infant Achilles in the River Styx. Those magic waters would make every part of him invulnerable; except the heel by which she held him.

The fairest woman in these ancient times was Helen, wife of Menelaus king of Sparta. Paris, Prince of Troy, while a guest of King Menelaus, fell in love with Helen. Aided by Aphrodite (Venus), goddess of love, Paris carried Helen away to his own realm. Menelaus declared war on Troy, and called on all his brother chieftains to battle.

Achilles, now a man of great beauty and courage, prepared to join Menelaus. Despite his mother's entreaties, Achilles, with his faithful followers the Myrmidons, joined the Greeks and their great fleet of a thousand ships. They set sail for Troy and a war that would last nine long years. Telephus, the son of mighty Hercules attempted to prevent the Greeks from landing on the coast of Mysia. While in combat he stumbled over a vine and fell, whereupon Achilles wounded him deeply with his spear. An oracle had once told Telephus he would be hurt in battle and that his wound could only be cured by the one who had inflicted it. In spite of his injury, he made his way to the Greek camp.

Meanwhile, the Greeks had learnt from an oracle that without the aid of Telephus, they would not be able to reach Troy. When Telephus arrived at the encampment, Achilles was called and shown the wound. He said: "The oracle has spoken truly, Telephus. I will heal your wound if you will show us the way to Troy." Telephus, realizing he had no choice but to agree to the bargain, answered: "If you can heal me, I will show you the way." Now Achilles had discovered a herb of great healing powers, *Achillea* or yarrow. He scraped rust from his spear and took the herb to form a mixture which he rubbed into the wound. The flow of blood stopped at once and the wound was cured. Telephus honoured his pact with Achilles and revealed to the Greeks the road to Troy. The prophecy so dreaded by Thetis finally came to pass. Paris shot a fatal poisoned arrow at Achilles' vulnerable heel. Hence the origin of the saying: "Achilles heel", which means a small but fatal weakness.

Yarrow has earned its generic name of *Achillea* from the Achilles legend. *Millefolium* refers to the dense, close-growing feathery leaves. *Achillea millefolium* comes in various hues but is most often white, and blooms from summer to fall (autumn). The common name "yarrow" derives from the Anglo-Saxon gaere; other traditional common names are staunch-weed, woundwort, knight's milfoil, and carpenter's wort. This last name refers to the healing properties of yarrow when it is used on wood-carvers' and carpenters' injuries.

YARROW *(Achillea millefolium)*

13

AJAX AND AJAX'S LARKSPUR

(Delphinium ajacis)

AJAX WAS an outstanding figure in the Trojan War, whose bravery made him a hero second only to his friend, Achilles.

The Trojan War raged for nine years. During that time, Achilles' devoted mother, Thetis, fearing her son's safety, hastened to Hephaestus (Vulcan), the lame god of fire, the forge and volcanic eruption. She requested that he create an impregnable suit of armour for her son. At once, the god fabricated a shield, a gold-crested helmet, a corselet (for the top half of his body), and greaves (to protect the shins), all of flawless workmanship. Thetis descended to earth and gave it to Achilles. The celestial suit moulded to his body and protected him from death during many fierce encounters with the enemy. But even it, with all its magical qualities, could not save him from the poisoned arrow aimed by Paris at Achilles' vulnerable heel.

Achilles body was retrieved by Ajax and the Greek hero Odysseus (known to the Romans as Ulysses). Desolate but proud, Thetis decreed that the Greeks should bestow the shining battle suit on the hero judged to be the most deserving. Odysseus and Ajax were the only contestants. A select group of chieftains finally awarded the prize to Odysseus, thereby placing his wisdom before Ajax's courage. Ajax was so distressed by the decision that he went insane, and later killed himself.

As Ajax lay dying his blood sank into the earth, and a flower, the larkspur (*Delphinium ajacis*), sprang from the ground. It bore on its leaves the first two letters of the name Ajax, Ai, the Greek word for "woe".

The common names of *D. ajacis* are Ajax's larkspur, garden larkspur, and field or forking larkspur. Sometimes poets writing about the god's death represent the plant as the hyacinth. Ajax's larkspur is a pretty but poisonous annual plant reaching a height of $2^1/2$ feet (1 metre). It blooms in mid-summer, and its blue or purple flowers are distinguished by an upward curving spur which grows behind the petals.

Right: AJAX'S LARKSPUR (*Delphinium ajacis*)

14

APHRODITE, ADONIS AND THE RED ANEMONE

(Adonis annua)

APHRODITE (VENUS) was the goddess of beauty, love, and marriage. The peerless rose and fragrant myrtle were her sacred plants. Swans, doves, sparrows and swallows, her special birds, were her messengers and transporters. In the most poetic legend of Aphrodite's birth, she first appeared, fully grown, on a delicate scallop shell floating on the sea. Sea foam carried her to the shore, where the Four Seasons awaited her. They attired the lovely maiden and led her to the immortals assembled on Mount Olympus. All were enchanted by Aphrodite's exquisite face and form, and by her graceful bearing and manner. Each god wanted her for his wife. Zeus (Jupiter), however, bestowed her upon Hephaestus (Vulcan), the lame god of fire, the forge and volcanic eruption, in gratitude for the thunderbolts he had created.

Aphrodite did not care for her new husband and deserted him for Ares (Mars), the dark and handsome god of war. The love between Aphrodite and Ares was ardent, and several beautiful children were born of their union – a daughter, Harmonia, who married King Cadmus of Thebes, and two sons, Eros (Cupid), male god of love, and Anteros, god of passion. The sensual goddess was generous with her attentions: the word "aphrodisiac", deriving from Aphrodite's name, means a stimulant that arouses sexual potency. Among her lovers was Anchises, Prince of Troy, to whom she bore a brave son, Aeneus; and several Olympian gods.

Aphrodite is said to have first appeared on a delicate scallop shell floating on the sea

Aphrodite's passion for Adonis, an unusually handsome mortal youth of muscular physique, was all consuming. Beside him, the rest of her life paled to insignificance. Adonis was a bold young hunter, happiest when in pursuit of dangerous game. Aphrodite joined him in the chase dressed like Artemis (Diana), the huntress; but she was concerned about the danger he was in from the fiercer wild animals. She pleaded with him to hunt only deer and hare; his pursuit of bears, wolves and boars could result in his death, a possibility she found unbearable. Adonis laughingly took no notice, and escaped from her rose-scented bower to join his friends in their chosen sport.

During the pursuit of a powerful wild boar, Adonis threw his spear and wounded the creature. In pain, it turned and thrust its sharp tusks into the hunter before trampling on him. Aphrodite heard Adonis' dying moans. She commanded her white swans to draw her chariot swiftly to where her lover lay. But she was to find Adonis already dead, his blood soaking into the earth. Her tears mingled with his blood as the grief-stricken goddess vowed, "As an eternal token of my grief, Adonis, each year your blood will be transformed into flowers." Shortly afterwards, the crimson blossoms of the red anemone (*Adonis annua*) sprang from the ground on that very spot. Like Adonis, the red anemone, or windflower is short lived – the wind blows the flowers open and then puffs the petals away.

Aphrodite begged Zeus to allow Adonis to return to her from the Underworld. Her request was granted on the condition that he should spend half the year – fall (autumn) and winter – with Hades (Pluto) and Persephone (Proserpina), King and Queen of the Shades. (For Persephone's tale, see "Demeter: Agriculture and Corn" later in this chapter.) Spring and summer, by Zeus' decree, would free Adonis to be reunited with his goddess of love and beauty. So myth aligns itself with Nature's changing seasons – the withering and death of plants in cold weather and their resurgence in spring, when crimson anemones bloom and Adonis emerges to meet his beloved.

> *By this, the boy that by her side lay kill'd*
> *Was melted like a vapour from her sight,*
> *And in his blood that on the ground lay spill'd,*
> *A purple flower sprung up, chequer'd with white;*
> *Resembling well his pale cheeks, and the blood*
> *Which in round drops upon their whiteness stood.*

WILLIAM SHAKESPEARE
Venus and Adonis

THE FLOWER OF APHRODITE, THE ROSE

(Rosa spp.*)*

IT IS SAID that the rose displays the most perfect and harmonious development of the plant form. Known as "the queen of flowers", it is aptly attributed to the goddess of love and beauty, who has been worshipped under many names in disparate civilizations – as Ishtar, Astarte, Semiramis, Isis and Venus, all having similar attributes to the Grecian Aphrodite. The rose is indigenous to several continents, and there are countless legends surrounding it, both pagan and Christian. Statues of Aphrodite are traditionally garlanded with roses, and her worshippers ensure that roses adorn her shrines. The origin of the rose is often given as the time when the ocean bore Aphrodite on sea foam to the shore. It is believed that the earth, in gratitude for her birth, simultaneously brought forth this queen of flowers to pay homage to her.

Wild roses were usually single, a rare, honeyed fragrance emanating from them. They were surrounded with protective thorns, and grew thickly in tangled masses. When Aphrodite hastened to the dying Adonis after her chariot had touched the ground, she ran in desperation through thorny rose bushes covered in white flowers. The thorns tore her feet and, while she ran, her blood stained the roses crimson. As the story goes, some wild roses have remained red ever since.

APHRODITE'S TREE, MYRTLE

(Myrtus communis)

Fragrant myrtle was sacred to Aphrodite, and sprays of myrtle blossoms, twined together, made a delicate chaplet or wreath for the goddess's brow. She owned a magic girdle, and whoever wore it became an object of love and desire. Myrtle has a reputation for being an aphrodisiac; linked with love and feminine allure, aromatic myrtle is included in a bride's wedding bouquet in some regions of the Mediterranean.

It grows as an evergreen shrub or tree, and its pointed green leaves are glossy and sweetly scented. The plant bears perfumed blooms in mid- to late summer, and each tiny white-petalled flower is almost hidden by a puff of prominent golden stamens. The tightly folded white buds burst open in a day.

21

APOLLO, DAPHNE AND THE BAY TREE
(Laurus nobilis)

APOLLO OR Phoebus Apollo was the son of Leto (Latona) and of Zeus (Jupiter), supreme ruler of all Olympian deities. Born on the island of Delos, Apollo was the god of light, poetry, music and prophecy. Phoebus means 'shining, bright and pure', and Apollo became identified with Helios (Sol), the sun god who drove his sun-chariot across the sky. His chaste twin, Artemis (Diana), was the moon goddess.

"Most Greek of all gods" was Apollo. In sculpture, representations of his form have long been seen as the ideal of male beauty. He was loved by both youths and maidens, often with unhappy consequences.

The greatest temple dedicated to the god was at Delphi. Here, seekers of Truth asked questions which were delivered to Apollo, Lord of the Delphic oracle, by a high priestess. The patron of music, often playing on his golden lyre, Apollo was also the god of philosophy and of archery. At one time he was the god of healing, before the birth of his son, Asclepius (Aesculapius), who took on this role in his stead. The slayer of the terrible dragon-serpent, Python, at Delphi, Apollo was strong and fearless; the poet Homer called him the "far-darting archer". Dolphins were particularly sacred to him.

One of the Seven Wonders of the Ancient World, the famous Colossus of Rhodes, is thought to have been a statue of Apollo, the sun god.

Apollo –
...The Lord of the unerring bow,
The God of life, and poesy, and light –
The Sun in human limbs array'd, and brow
All radiant from his triumph in the fight.

LORD BYRON

Apollo in The Chariot of the Sun

Daphne was to be Apollo's first love. She was a fair and graceful nymph, daughter of the river god Peneus. She delighted in woodland sports, roaming among the pine and olive trees in her secluded world. She ignored the many lovers who sought her, abhorring any thought of marriage. She wished to remain virginal like Artemis (see "Artemis and Wormwood").

One day Eros (Cupid), the male god of love and son of Aphrodite (Venus), goddess of beauty and love, was in a mischievous and vengeful mood, the result of a disparaging remark made by Apollo. He stood on Mount Parnassus, selected two darts from his quiver and took aim. One was a gold-tipped arrow to excite amorous passion, this he chose to pierce the heart of Apollo. The second arrow pierced Daphne's heart, but this was lead tipped, designed to repel those feelings of love.

Apollo glimpsed Daphne running through the green forest. Immediately seized with an overpowering desire for her, he gave chase. Daphne fled on wings of fear, her long hair flowing freely, her garments sweeping around her shapely limbs. Apollo followed, ever more entranced, beseeching her to stop and listen to his declarations of love. He exclaimed, "I am the god of medicine and know the virtue of all healing plants, but cannot cure my own malady." These words only made the nymph run more quickly, but she was becoming exhausted. Apollo was moving closer and soon she could feel his panting breath. Her strength failed; she was ready to sink to the ground. In a last desperate gesture, her arms outstretched, she called to her father Peneus.

Suddenly, her lovely body began to transform into tender enclosing bark. Her hair became scented leaves, her arms branches, and her feet penetrated the earth as roots. The nymph, Daphne, had become the fragrant, evergreen bay laurel tree (*Laurus nobilis*). Incredulous, Apollo embraced and kissed the new bark, able to feel the trembling flesh beneath. He told Daphne that, as she could not be his wife, she would be his tree, and he would wear her leaves as his crown. Since this time, the leaves of the bay laurel have been woven into wreaths to crown outstanding achievers, whether in sport, government, war, or literature. It is from this practice that the title 'Poet Laureate' derives.

Right: Bay Tree *(Laurus nobilis)*

APOLLO AND CLYTIE, AND THE SUNFLOWER

(Calendula arvensis and *C. officinalis)*

The marigold that goes to bed wi' th' sun
And with him rises weeping.

WILLIAM SHAKESPEARE
The Winter's Tale

CLYTIE WAS a lovely water nymph who fell deeply in love with the god Apollo. He was indifferent to her feelings and could not return her love. The heartbroken nymph pined away, sitting on the ground day and night, her hair falling around her shoulders as she wept. She would not eat a morsel of food, and for nine days sat gazing up at the sun

Above: GARDEN MARIGOLD *(Calendula officinalis)*

26

god as he rose in the morning. All day she would turn her face in his direction until his sun-chariot completed its course. Finally the gods took pity on Clytie and changed her into a sunflower. Her neck became the stem, holding up the flower that follows the sun during his journey across the sky until he vanishes in the evening.

The plant we know as the sunflower today *(Helianthus annus)* is native to Mexico and Peru and was not introduced to Europe until the 16th century. It is the Greek wild marigold *(Calendula arvensis,* similar to the garden marigold *C. officinalis)* that is believed to be the sunflower of legend. Many writers, including Ovid, have alluded to its affinity with the sun.

Calendula, known to the ancient Greeks, is also known to Arabian and Indian cultures, where it symbolizes life, eternity, and health.

> *It openeth his Flower and turneth round all day after the*
> *Sun and closeth in his golden beames at night.*
>
> Dr Bullein, E. S. Rohde
> *Gardens of Delight*

Old names for the marigold, almost forgotten today, are "sunflower", "gold", "rudde", and "pot marigold". It was once an emblem of obedience and constancy, the latter meaning being adopted by lovers in their flower messages.

APOLLO, HYACINTHUS AND THE ROMAN HYACINTH

(Hyacinthus orientalis)

APOLLO BECAME attached to a beautiful youth called Hyacinthus. Always by the youth's side, Apollo carried the nets when Hyachinthus went fishing, went with him on his excursions into the high mountains, and led his dogs when he hunted. Apollo was so enthralled with his companion that he forgot to play his golden lyre or let fly his silver arrows.

Zephyrus, the West Wind, also loved Hyacinthus, and was jealous of the close relationship between the handsome god and the fair youth. One day Apollo was teaching the boy the art of discus throwing. Apollo held the discus high, and with strength and skill sent it flying far into the air. Hyacinthus, in a hurry to retrieve the plate, ran forward, and Zephyrus took his revenge. The discus hit the earth, but before Hyacinthus could grasp it, the West Wind blew the stone plate upwards and dashed it against the youth's forehead.

Hyacinthus dropped to the ground, bleeding and deathly pale. The distressed Apollo tried to staunch the wound with his healing art. But his efforts were to no avail – the cut was too deep. The boy died in Apollo's arms. The god fell to weeping, and said, "Would that I could die for thee! But as this could not be I will keep your memory alive playing my lyre and singing of thee, and thou shalt become my flower."

Hyacinthus' blood flowed red on the green grass. Apollo changed the fallen blood into clusters of crimson flowers, the petals inscribed with the Greek word meaning "Alas". Zephyrus, perceiving the fatal effect of his jealousy, was repentant; he lingered to caress the delicate flowers that had sprung from the young man's blood.

The hyacinth *(Hyacinthus orientalis)* is one of the most scented spring flowers. The ancient story of Hyacinthus, like that of Adonis, celebrates spring vegetation and recognises the preciousness of its limited life, withering as it does with the coming of autumn.

Or they might watch the quoit-pitchers, intent
On either side, pitying the sad death
Of Hyacinthus, when the cruel breath
Of Zephyr slew him; Zephyr penitent,
Who now ere Phoebus mounts the firmament,
Fondles the flower amid the sobbing rain.

JOHN KEATS
Endymion

HYACINTH
(*Hyacinthus orientalis*)

APOLLO, CYPARISSUS AND THE CYPRESS TREE

(Cupressus sempervirens)

AFTER THE tragic death of his beloved friend Hyacinthus, Apollo found comfort in the companionship of an accomplished young hunter, Cyparissus, son of the hero Telephus.

This friendship though, would also prove to be one of tragedy. One cloudless summer's day the friends were hunting as usual when they saw a sudden trembling of branches in a thicket of bushes. Cyparissus took aim and threw his spear at the sunlit spot. The piercing cry of a stricken animal rang out as the weapon struck. Parting the leafy boughs, the god and the hunter saw Apollo's pet stag lying dead. Cyparissus was so distressed by this misfortune that he could think of nothing else. In his melancholia he refused to eat or drink, even when the most delicious food was offered to him. Ambrosial draughts, fragrant with restorative herbs, were put to his pale lips, but he refused even to taste them. Without nourishment and with no will to live, Cyparissus succumbed at last to death.

Once more Apollo had lost a friend dear to his heart. Before Cyparissus was laid in the earth, Apollo vowed, "Your body will be changed into a tree that shall be named after you, the 'cypress', and it shall be grown to shade the graves of those who were greatly loved."

The cypress is linked to Hades (Pluto), god of the Underworld, for Apollo had decreed that it was to signify mourning for the dead. True to Apollo's wishes, cypress trees are planted as a sign of mourning, and their leafy stems are bound into wreaths.

Above: CYPRESS *(Cupressus sempervirens)*

30

ARTEMIS AND WORMWOOD

(Artemisia absinthium)

But lo! from high Hymettus to the plain,
The queen of night asserts her silent reign.
No murky vapour, herald of the storm,
Hides her fair face, nor girds her glowing form...

LORD BYRON, GEORGE GORDON
The Corsair

ARTEMIS (DIANA), the huntress deity of the chase and goddess of the moon, was the child of Zeus and Leto and twin sister of Apollo. The twin gods were born on Mount Cynthus in the island of Delos–hence Artemis' other name, Cynthia.

Artemis was as beautiful as Apollo was handsome. The young of wild animals were sacred to her, especially deer. She is commonly depicted with a bow, a quiver full of arrows, a hunting dog or a stag by her side, and a crescent moon on her forehead.

Chaste and virginal, Artemis spurned the desires of gods and men. Though she was reputedly a maiden-divinity unconquered by love, a few stories dispute this image of a cold goddess.

It is said that Artemis loved the giant, Orion, son of Neptune, and Endymion, a mortal youth. With one of her arrows, Artemis accidentally killed Orion as he waded through the sea. In her sorrow, Artemis placed him and his dog, Sirius as constellations in the sky. Endymion grazed his flock of sheep on Mount Latmos. Each night Artemis watched the beautiful youth sleeping and kissed him with her shining moonbeams. These caused Endymion to fall into an eternal sleep in which he would never grow old. She bore him to her sacred cave, where she caressed him from the heavens.

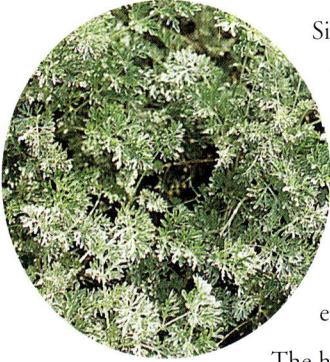

Silver-leafed wormwood was Artemis' particular herb, and she was responsible for plant growth and fertility. She was the first to discover the many benefits of wormwood, and in gratitude bestowed her name on this pungently scented plant family.

Prepared extracts of wormwood ease stomach disorders and help quell travel sickness. Herb lore states that wearing a few sprigs of wormwood when travelling, putting a soft leaf in each shoe, or fastening a small branch to the mode of transport will ensure a tireless and safe journey.

The huntress goddess, Artemis may have esteemed the herb for this reason too – her devotees of the chase remained fresh and tireless if they wore sprays of wormwood.

Some myths declare that "Dittany of Crete" (*Origanum dictamus*) is another herb dedicated to Artemis, goddess of the moon and of hunting. Its association with the huntress-deity is due to the strange power dittany has of drawing out splinters of wood, thorns and arrows from the body – a boon to all hunters. Literature of past centuries testifies to this phenomenon, giving accounts of cases where arrows were drawn from wounds after distilled dittany was applied to the affected area as a poultice. Other historical records relate the observation that, if goats were wounded with arrows that remained in their flesh, grazing on dittany would cause the arrows to fall out.

Above: WORMWOOD *(Artemesia absinthium)* and DITTANY *(Origanum dictamus)*

Artemis (Diana), goddess of the moon and of hunting.

ATHENE
AND THE OLIVE TREE
(Olea europaea)

Yet are thy skies as blue, thy crags as wild;
Sweet are thy groves, and verdant are thy fields,
Thine olive ripe as when Minerva smiled …

GEORGE GORDON, LORD BYRON
Childe Harold's Pilgrimage

PALLAS ATHENE (Minerva), the virgin goddess of wisdom, practical skills and prudent warfare was the favourite child of Zeus, ruler of Olympus. She had sprung from his head fully mature and radiant in full armor, he her only parent.

Her bird was the owl, her plant the olive tree. As patroness of the arts and trades, Athene presided over agriculture and navigation, and spinning, weaving and needlework. Although depicted as a war-like goddess, she was not an aggressor, but a fierce protector of her territory.

During the reign of Cecrops, the first king of a great city in Greece, Poseidon, god of the sea and Pallas Athena contended for possession of that city. The gods on Mount Olympus decreed that it should be awarded to whichever deity produced the gift most useful to mortals. Poseidon presented the world with the horse and explained how it would benefit humankind. Then Athena caused an olive tree to grow.

She described the manifold uses to which its wood, fruit, oil, foliage and twigs could be applied. Then she proclaimed that the olive was the sign of peace and prosperity. The gods judged that the olive was the most serviceable gift to the world of mortals, and awarded the prize to Athene. From then on, the city was known as Athens.

Athene, virgin goddess of wisdom and warfare, taming the Centaur

The olive tree may last for several hundred years. When at last the trunk is completely cut away, shoots appear at the base from a new stem, earning the tree the reputation of being immortal, like Athene. Her unique gift has a diversity of benefits for all Mediterranean people, who rely on the fruit and the pressed oil as a staple food, as medicine and as fuel for lamps.

DEMETER,
AND AGRICULTURE AND CORN;
PERSEPHONE,
AND VEGETATION AND SPRING

Demeter, goddess of agriculture

DEMETER (CERES), golden goddess of agriculture and corn, was one of the supreme Greek deities of the earth. A daughter of two Titans, Cronus and Rhea, she was also a sister of Zeus (Jupiter). To Zeus, she bore Persephone (Proserpina), goddess of vegetation and spring.

Persephone was a joyous, pretty girl, and when free of her duties helping her mother, gathered flowers with her friends on her favourite island, Sicily. One sunny day in the perpetual spring weather, she and her companions were wandering in the wooded vale of Enna, which was starred with blooms. Persephone glimpsed in the grass a shimmering carpet of flowers of a kind she had not seen before. Wishing to add a few of them to her collection of violets, many-hued crocuses and poppies, she ran from her merry companions to gather the blossoms for her basket.

Hades (Pluto), stern god of the Underworld, saw Persephone in the distance with her friends. Struck by her grace and fresh beauty, he left his chariot and went quietly to a screen of bushes from where he could see her more closely. He found himself overcome with love for Demeter's daughter. Knowing that her mother would never consent to a union which would place Persephone with shadowy beings in the darkness below the bright earth, he decided that abduction could be his only course.

As Persephone knelt among the flowers, an iron chariot drawn by four coal-black horses thundered toward her. Dark Hades was quickly at her side. He briskly lifted her into his chariot. The frightened maiden screamed for her friends and, in the struggle to free herself of the iron grasp, spilled her flowers onto the ground. Her comrades tried to rescue her, terrified though they were, and pleaded with Hades to set Persephone free. The terrible god struck the earth a tremendous blow with his two-pronged fork, making an enormous hole in the ground. Then, shouting to his steeds, he plunged headlong into the deep gloom of the lower world, Persephone in his tight grip.

Later that day, at sunset, Demeter returned home from the fields of ripening grain, pleased that all was going well with the crops. Persephone was not there to greet her, and Demeter sat down to wait. Evening came, the stars shone and Artemis in her full moonlit glory silvered the midnight sky.

When Eos (Aurora), the rosy-fingered goddess of the dawn, flashed across the sky heralding the coming of Apollo in his sun-chariot, Demeter knew that her beloved daughter had disappeared. She found the scattered flowers where they had fallen as Hades stole her daughter away, and so began her search.

She travelled a long time in her search for Persephone, disguised as a beggar-woman. When people were kind to the old woman, not knowing she was the goddess Demeter, she revealed her true rank, appearing in her shining garments, and rewarded them. And those who repulsed her, she severely punished.

While Demeter was preoccupied with her sad mission, the earth suffered from her lack of ministrations. No rain fell to refresh the plants or the grass, the sun's fierce rays withered the crops, and famine threatened. Humans prayed to the gods for help.

Demeter learnt from the sun god that it was Hades who had carried her daughter away. Hades had made Persephone his Queen, and she sat beside him on a gilded throne, majestic and solemn.

The anxious mother hurried to Olympus. She begged Zeus to return Persephone to her. If he would do this, she said, she would again replenish the earth. Zeus agreed, provided Persephone had not eaten during her stay in the lower regions. He sent his messenger Hermes (Mercury) to bring her back.

Hades consented to release Persephone. But he had already given her six pomegranate seeds to eat, knowing if she took food, he would not lose her completely. Hermes returned Persephone to her mother and, overjoyed, Demeter caused the earth to bloom again.

But Zeus' command had to be obeyed, and Persephone was obliged to return to her husband, clad in her sable vestments, pale and regal, six months of every year. The earth mourned her departure, and the skies were overcast. No crops grew until Persephone appeared above ground for her six months with Demeter. Then the skies cleared to a sunny blue, new shoots appeared on the earth, trees put out tender young leaves, flowers bloomed, and birds sang.

So in this pleasant vale we stand again,
The field of Enna, now once more ablaze
With flowers that brighten as thy footstep falls,
All flowers—but for one black blur of earth
Left by that closing chasm, thro' which the car
of dark Aidoneus rising rapt thee hence.

ALFRED, LORD TENNYSON
Demeter and Persephone

Some philosophical writers compare the disappearance and return of Persephone to the burial of a person's body and the immortality of his or her soul. Scholars write that the meaning of this legend is a vegetative one. Persephone, who is carried off to the Lower World, is the seed-core, which remains concealed in the ground until the maiden of spring returns to her mother. The seed then germinates, and new growth rises from the soil and ripens as grain crops.

In works of art, Demeter is crowned with a wreath of corn-ears, or a poppy, and holds a sceptre. In ancient times, Demeter's "corn" signified all cereal crops, including wheat and barley which, it is recorded, originated in the antique hills of the Fertile Crescent, from Syria and Turkey to Iran, where the primitive ancestors of later cereals grew in oak-forest clearings. Cereals formed the basis of civilization: from them came life-sustaining foods providing carbohydrates in the form of starches, and the sun-charged grains contained proteins, oils and salts – they were the foundation of a staple diet for humans, and provided feed for stock.

Agriculture became established as people learned to sow and harvest grain-seed. It was an autumnal rite for the farmer of ancient Greece to pray to the corn goddess when he buried grain in prepared earth; he rejoiced when he had reaped the harvest of ripe crops and brought back the yellow sheaves to the threshing floor. He gave the beneficent goddess a thanks offering by making a rustic image of her beside a heap of golden grain on the threshing floor, with cornstalks and poppies in her hands.

As goddess of agriculture and corn, Demeter was often depicted with corn and poppies in her hands. It is probable that the brilliant red corn poppy (*Papaver rhoeas*), or field poppy, was Demeter's poppy. It grows wild among crops and on arable land in exuberant profusion, as well as on roadsides.

However, it may be the opium poppy (*Papaver somniferum*) that was associated with the goddess. She well knew somniferum's sleep-inducing properties, and used it for this purpose in some of her magical practices. The opium poppy has grown wild in the Mediterranean since time immemorial. The flowers are red, silvery-white or lilac with pink or purple markings and the stems and leaves are large and grey-blue.

DIONYSUS
AND THE GRAPE VINE *(Vitis vinifera)*
AND IVY *(Hedera helix)*

THE GREEK god of the grape vine was Dionysus (Bacchus). Ivy was also sacred to him, and his animals were the dolphin, serpent, lynx, leopard, panther and donkey. Dionysus was born prematurely in the tumult of an inferno. His mortal mother died in the chaos, and his immortal father rescued him from the flames.

In mythology, Zeus (Jupiter), father of the gods and supreme over them all, could never resist the charms of beautiful women, whether they were goddesses, nymphs, or mortals. This caused his wife, Hera (Juno), goddess of marriage and motherhood, extreme jealousy, so she was always plotting revenge on his unfortunate lovers and their offspring.

Zeus had become the devoted lover of a beautiful Theban princess, Semele. One day he told her he would grant her dearest wish. Hera having put the idea into the princess's head, Semele requested that she behold Zeus in all his glory, with his thunderbolts, as king of the gods. Zeus tried to dissuade her, knowing that no mortal could survive the experience. But Semele persisted.

Zeus had given his word, and so, arraying himself in less than his usual splendor, entered Semele's chamber in dazzling radiance. Although the god had dimmed his glory, Semele's human frame was overwhelmed by the brilliance. She perished from the shock, but not before giving premature birth to a son, Dionysus. The palace burned to ashes in the fire caused by the lightning flashing around Zeus.

40

Fearing Hera's vengeful nature and her desire to harm Semele's son, Zeus snatched up the tiny baby and sewed him into his thigh, keeping him there until the infant was strong enough to survive. When the time came, Zeus directed his messenger, Hermes (Mercury), to carry Dionysus to the Nysian nymphs, to be nourished by them until he was grown to young manhood.

Zeus rewarded the nymphs by placing them in the sky among the stars as a constellation called the Hyades. He declared his great love for Semele by raising her spirit to the rank of a deity.

Dionysus grew up to be a beautiful young man. While still a youth he discovered the culture of the vine. His guide and tutor was Silenus, often depicted as a satyr (half man, half goat), and sometimes as an inebriated old man riding on an ass.

Dionysus travelled far and wide to many countries, even to India, where he is said to have stayed for several years. Wherever he went he taught humans the art of making wine from the fruit of the grape vine. A large band of followers gathered around him – Silenus on his donkey, wood nymphs, centaurs (half man, half horse), satyrs, and riotous young women called "bacchantes". The merry throng crowned with ivy leaves drank the wine they had made from grapes, water and sunshine. They danced, sang, and played musical instruments as they progressed from place to place. Leading them was Dionysus himself, riding in a chariot drawn by lithe black panthers or elegant spotted leopards.

Many adventures befell Dionysus on his extensive wanderings. One of the most famous tales involves his capture by pirates. The god was asleep, alone on the sandy shore of an island, when sailors on a pirate ship caught sight of the handsome youth with long dark hair. They decided to seize the sleeping boy, take him on board, and sell him as a slave in Asia.

Left: The sea voyage of Dionysus

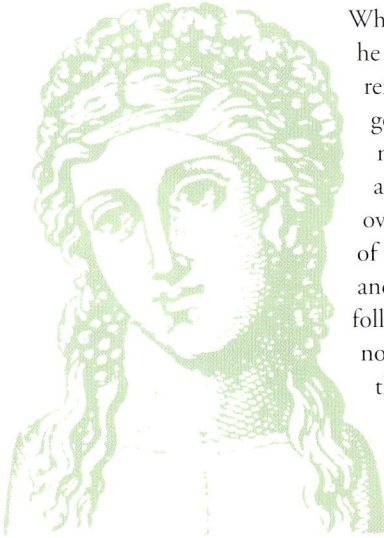

When Dionysus awoke and found himself at sea, he ordered the crew to take him to Naxos. They refused, and continued to row on. At once the god caused vines laden with grapes to run up the mast, and ivy to twine thickly around the oars and under the vessel. The ship could not move, overgrown as it was with thick foliage. The sound of flutes, clinking cymbals, and revelry was heard, and then all the bacchantes and Dionysus' other followers climbed onto the ship. The sailors by now were overcome with terror and jumped into the sea, where they were metamorphosed into dolphins. The helmsman alone was saved – he had already opposed the pirates' evil plan. Dionysus said to him, "Steer the ship to Naxos, and no harm will come to you."

Dionysus was now established as a divinity and god of the grape vine. He is depicted wearing a chaplet of vine leaves and bunches of grapes entwined with ivy.

Scholars have written that Dionysus may be seen as symbolic of both the productive and the intoxicating power of nature: "Life-giving, healing every ill." Wine as a beverage has been one of people's greatest pleasures, as well as having diverse ritualistic and symbolic significance. The virtues of Nature's vintage have been extolled in books, songs, poetry and art. A dedicated connoisseur once compared the scent of grape-flowers on a sunny day to the bouquet of the mature wine.

Dionysus's greatest love was Ariadne, a beautiful princess of Crete whom he found alone and weeping on the island of Naxos. After her death Dionysus took her crown and threw it high into the heavens, where it remains to this day as the constellation known as "Ariadne's Crown".

Ivy (*Hedera helix*) was also dedicated to Dionysus, whose crown of vine was entwined with ivy leaves. His followers wore ivy wreaths, and bound the plant around their staffs. It was believed that ivy prevented intoxication. But if intoxication did occur, an infusion of bruised ivy leaves should be taken, thereby removing the effects of over-indulgence. Signs with painted ivy bushes were once hung above tavern doors to symbolize the good quality of the wine within. Today, ivy is known as poisonous, and should not be taken internally.

IVY *(Hedera helix)*

ECHO AND NARCISSUS
AND THE NARCISSUS FLOWER
(Narcissus tazetta)

THERE WAS once a talkative young wood nymph called Echo who, while she danced, sang and chattered with other nymphs, always managed to have the last word. She and the woodland sprites roamed over hills and through forests, and bathed in cool streams. They often glimpsed Narcissus hunting with his companions, and Echo became captivated by his beauty and grace.

Narcissus was the son of Cephissus and Liriope. A youth whose great pleasure was to hunt in the woods with his comrades, Narcissus had no desire to become attached to any of the maidens who gathered around him with adoration.

The day came when Echo could remain silent no longer. She approached Narcissus and declared her love for him. Startled by her forwardness, Narcissus replied, "I cannot pledge my love to you, go away." Echo was mortified by his cruelty; she entreated Aphrodite to punish him by making him feel the pain of unrequited love.

But Echo's unmaidenly conduct displeased the gods. They said she must depart the woodland groves forever, to haunt solitary places and rocky bluffs. Her destiny was to repeat the last sound she heard, thereby always having the final word.

Full of sorrow, the nymph wandered away to sit by herself on stony outcrops and in mountain caves. She pined away for love of Narcissus until all that remained of her was her musical voice.

Right: NARCISSUS FLOWER, *(Narcissus lazetta)*

46

Aphrodite pitied poor Echo, and had not forgotten the nymph's plea for Narcissus' punishment. One day the youth was hunting as usual. It was a prolonged chase, and he was hot and thirsty. Seeing a clear pool, he knelt down, bent over, and cupped his hands to drink. He saw a bewitching face looking up at him from the shining water, and he was overcome with admiration. Thinking he had seen a lovely water nymph, he bent over with his arms outstretched to catch her; but the pool shimmered and the figure dissolved. In love for the first time, Narcissus persisted in trying to catch the elusive creature, for by now he was carried away with desire. He did not realise it was himself he saw in the mirror-like pond.

He stayed by the pool day and night, unable to tear himself away from the beloved but elusive form; even in the moonlight the image gazed back at him with longing. Echo stayed near Narcissus all the time. He could not see her, but when he cried, "Ah! How sad!", Echo repeated, "Sad."

The despairing lover, neither eating nor drinking, wasted away, until finally he died at the pool's edge. Tearful wood nymphs came to bury him, calling "Woe! Woe!" Echo repeated, "Woe!" When the nymphs reached the grassy bank by the pool, Narcissus was not there. Instead, the gods had metamorphosed him into an exquisite flower bearing the name Narcissus. It is said that the flower flourishes best beside sequestered pools that reflect its pale likeness.

The Narcissus flower referred to in this sad myth is *Narcissus tazetta,* a native wildflower of the Mediterranean. The term "Narcissus complex" has come into our language to describe an obsessive preoccupation with one's own good looks.

Narcissus was bewitched by the face looking up at him from the shining water

GANYMEDE AND TANSY

(Tanacetum vulgare originally *'Athanasia')*

And godlike Ganymede, most beautiful
Of men; the gods beheld and caught him up
To heaven, so beautiful was he, to pour
The wine to Jove, and ever dwell with them.

HOMER
Bryant's translation

HEBE, GODDESS of youth, was Zeus' personal attendant and cup bearer to the gods, until she was dismissed after falling during a solemn occasion.

To search for another cup bearer to pour the sacred nectar, Zeus assumed the form of an eagle. He flew over the earth and saw Ganymede, son of a king of Troy. The youth, the most beautiful of mortal men, was with friends on Mount Ida. The eagle flew down and, clutching the young man in his talons, carried him off to Mount Olympus, dwelling place of the gods.

Zeus commanded Hermes (Mercury), messenger of the gods, to take Ganymede away to be made immortal. He said, "When he has tasted immortality, let him return to us."

A herb with eternal properties was given to Ganymede. We know this herb as tansy (*Tanacetum vulgare*); the Greek word for it is "Athanasia", meaning immortality. The long-lasting golden button-flowers gave rise to the herb's reputation for being deathless, as did the preserving powers of tansy's aromatic, feathery leaves. The leaves were used by the ancients, together with other herbs and spices, to embalm the dead.

Ganymede remained in the service of Zeus as his cup-bearer at celestial banquets, and later was identified with the spirit of the sources of the Nile. As such he was placed among the constellations as Aquarius or the water-carrier.

50

There, too, flushed Ganymede, his rosy thigh
Half buried in the eagle's down,
Sole as a flying star shot through the sky
Above the pillared town.

TENNYSON
The Palace of Art

TANSY *(Tanacetum vulgare)*

FLORA
FLOWERS AND SPRING

FLORA, THE ROMAN goddess of flowers and the spring, wore a garland of scented blossoms on her brow. She loved and married the god of the west wind, Zephyrus. He carried her gently with him, she scattering flowers along the way. The earth glowed in all the colours of the rainbow.

Flowers bloomed everywhere. Rocky crevices that had been grey and bare in winter now glistened with vivid shades: red anemones blazed on the ground; roses tumbled over rocks; pinks, hyacinths, irises, crocuses, campanula, poppies and white spring heather were seen in unexpected places. Blue speedwells, purple violets, and wild red strawberries carpeted woods and forests; pastel primulas sheeted meadows. On mountain tops, in fissures and narrow clefts, and on craggy slopes, wild thyme, oregano, sage, rosemary, rue, lavender, chamomile, basil, balm, pimpernel, wormwood, yarrow, and countless other herbs flourished – their fragrance filled the air and the honey-bees swarmed.

In Roman times, an annual festival, the Floralia, was held in Flora's honor from 28 April until 3 May each year, with a great deal of merriment. In Helston, Cornwall, a holiday was observed on 8 May, known as "Flora Day"; it is thought that the custom was a survival of the ancient Roman Floralia. Boughs of flowering hawthorn were gathered, and the ancient Flora Day Song was sung. Long lines of people, with hands joined, danced through the streets and open houses.

Left: Roman fresco of Flora, goddess of flowers and spring

POMONA,
ROMAN GODDESS OF ORCHARDS
AND GARDENS

POMONA, THE ROMAN goddess who watched over orchards and gardens, was slim and shapely; her lovely face had the apple glow of one who works at rural tasks. She was chaste and solitary, emulating her idol, Artemis, the huntress goddess. She dismissed many suitors, having no desire to share her full and happy life.

Vertumnus was the most ardent of all Pomona's admirers and not as easily rebuffed as the others. A Roman fruit deity connected with the changing seasons, Vertumnus presided over the transformation of plants and their progression from blossom to fruit. One day, the young god changed himself into an old crone. Dressed in a ragged skirt and shabby shawl, he knocked on the closed gate. Pomona opened it so the harmless old creature could enter. Seating himself under an apple tree while Pomona trimmed the branches, he said, "You are so enchanting and beautiful, why are you not married, my dear?"

Pomona answered, "I do not wish to share my life with anyone."

"Pretty one," the crone said. "There is a young man who loves you to distraction. His name is Vertumnus. Like you, he is happiest in gardens and orchards. You would be able to carry out your tasks with greater ease in the companionship of a loving husband."

Then Pomona confided, "I must admit that, among all my suitors, he alone is the only husband I could love." Vertumnus, shining with happiness, shed his disguise. He stood before Pomona in his true form: handsome and irresistible. Pomona was both stunned and entranced. As she had already revealed her feelings, she told him now that she also loved him.

Above: Pomona with her friend and idol the goddess Artemis

Vertumnus, Roman god of fruit, and Pomona, goddess of orchards and gardens

Pomona, as her name implies, was originally the apple-orchard deity, but she was also regarded as presiding over other fruits. Because Vertumnus nurtured blossoms, helping them to become fruit at the right season, he was a perfect partner for Pomona. They watched over orchards and gardens together, each utilizing their own skills. They are depicted holding pruning knives, shears, gardening tools, fruits, and flowers.

ANCIENT EGYPTIAN

Ancient Egypt holds for our time an air of mystery and magic. The land of pyramids, Pharaohs and the beautiful Cleopatra is rich in mythology and legend; it was, according to belief, populated by a large number of gods and goddesses.

The ruling god was Ra or Phra, who created human beings and the universe. Ra is said to have originated as the formless god Atum, enclosed in a lotus bud in the bosom of Nun who was Chaos, the primeval ocean. Ashtart was Egypt's goddess of love and fertility; she is depicted standing naked on a lion with a lotus flower in her hand.

Certain trees were regarded as sacred to the ancient Egyptians. Among them was the tamarisk with its slender branches and feathery clusters of tiny, pink flowers appealed to this culture's love of beauty. The gall-like fruits of the tamarisk were the weapon of Anu, god of the heavens, and were hung on doors along with date-palm branches to ward off evil spirits. The palm tree was a sacred symbol to Safekht, goddess of learning. Another hallowed tree was the Nile acacia.

Specimens of rare trees were brought back to ancient Egypt from other countries, their roots carefully embedded in large boxes of earth. They were replanted in the vast gardens of the Pharaohs and the rich and powerful ruling classes, and in the sacred groves of temples.

In the hot, dry desert of Egypt, the god of the Nile was relied on to flood the desert plains so the crops of corn and the orchards could flourish. Fruit and trees feature prominently in the ancient legends.

HATHOR
AND THE SYCAMORE FIG

(Ficus sycomorus)

T HE SYCAMORE fig *(Ficus sycomorus)* was a very significant, sacred tree dedicated to the goddess of fertility, Hathor. At Memphis, the ancient center of Lower Egypt, Hathor was worshipped as a tree goddess and called "the Lady of the Sycamore Tree". She was also regarded in Egyptian legend as the most famous of the cow goddesses. In addition, she was a sky goddess, the Eye of the sun god, Ra, and the personification of the sky itself. Between her horns she wore the sun's disk; her belly was the sky, and her hide and udders were the stars and planets. Hathor was originally depicted as a cow's head. The goddess later took on human form, but surviving images show her with the ears of a cow.

Hathor was often described as the Golden One, and as the goddess of love. The Greeks replaced her with Aphrodite, the goddess of love and beauty.

There are several legends about Hathor and the sycamore tree. Hathor lived in a counterpart of the sacred sycamore in the Afterlife; she would emerge from it to offer food and drink to the shades of the dead.

The young Pharaoh, Tutankhamun, linked himself with Hathor. He knew he would find refuge under her astral sycamore branches while she nourished him on his soul's journey. It was believed that he would recline on a subtle replica of the couch later found in his tomb. This piece of furniture was of elegant design, fashioned into the shape of two cows made of wood; the bodies were coated with plaster, gilded, and inlaid with trefoils of blue paste to

A 19th Dynasty Egyptian painting depicting Queen Nefertari and the Goddess Hathor

resemble the patches of colour on a cow's hide. Each animal wore the sun's disk between her horns. Among the fabled treasures of the King's burial chamber was a throne, the seat inlaid with ivory and ebony to resemble the hide of Hathor as the cow deity.

Because of the sycamore fig's ability to produce a great abundance of fruit, it seemed logical to regard the tree as sacred to the goddess of fertility. It was one of the largest and most common trees in Egypt, growing to a height of at least 9–12 metres (30–40 feet). It offered a welcome green canopy for people and animals, a shelter from the relentless rays of the Egyptian sun.

Known as "Pharaoh's fig", the sycamore fig produces figs on the trunk, and on old and new branches. The fruit is smaller than that of the ordinary fig *(Ficus carica)*, and a most useful food.

59

IMHOTEP
AND THE PAPYRUS PLANT
(Cyperus papyrus)

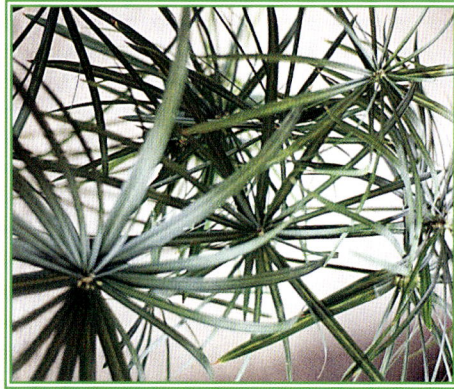

IMHOTEP WAS believed by the Egyptians to be the son of Ptah, the great "Creator-God", and a maiden called Khredu'ankh. But he was born a mortal who became a high official at King Djoser's court in the Early Old Kingdom of the Third Dynasty. Imhotep was the wisest of men, a sage, magician, scribe, architect, and physician. His wide range of achievements set him above all others, and he was elevated to the rank of god.

Imhotep was the patron of scribes. Surviving statuettes show him seated with a papyrus roll spread open on his knees. A temple at Sakkara was dedicated to Imhotep as foremost of scribes (he is said to have been the writer of several books no longer in existence). It was the custom of writers to honour Imhotep before they began work: after dipping their reed pens in the ink well, they would shake a few drops of ink to one side.

Above: PAPYRUS *(Cyperus papyrus)*

Believed to be the first architect of stone buildings, Imhotep is credited with having designed the Step Pyramid near Sakkara. A statue base near the entrance of the Pyramid is inscribed with Imhotep's name and titles. There is also a record that Imhotep built a temple at Edfu, using a plan that, he is reported to have said, "fell from heaven".

Imhotep's reputation as a healing god lived on. In the Late Period (716–332 BC), pilgrims, and especially the sick and crippled, came from all over Egypt to a temple dedicated to him at Sakkara. Shrines assigned to him are found in Karnak, Deir el-Medina and Philae, and many other temples. The Greeks called Imhotep "Imouthes", and identified him with their renowned physician, Asclepius.

It was Imhotep's role as scribe and architect, as designer of buildings on a grand scale, that brings to mind the materials he would have used in drawing up his plans. The papyrus roll, portrayed in statuettes of him, would have been painstakingly crafted by the Egyptians. Papyrus as paper is depicted in the shape of a long sheet rolled up at one end. Fragments of papyrus scrolls have been found in Egyptian tombs.

Previous sacred writings were graven on stone or produced on parchment. Parchment was made from sheep or goat skins; many processes were needed before powdered chalk or lime could be rubbed onto the surface to make it smooth. A cheaper, easier method for writing material had to be found; with papyrus the Egyptians discovered the way.

Papyrus plants *(Cyperus papyrus)* were sometimes referred to as bulrushes. They grew abundantly along the watery banks of the Nile, and were harvested for numerous purposes. For the making of paper, moistened strips of the lowest and thickest parts of the stem were peeled away, leaving the inner whitish pith, which was cut into slices and laid side by side to form the longitudinal warp; shorter strips were overlaid crosswise. The whole sheet was sun dried, and the writing surface polished. Ink of sepia animal charcoal, and other substances, was applied with a reed pen. These materials endured in literary use from the pyramid age, if not before, to the 4th century A.D., and were used intermittently up to 1250.

The papyrus plant can grow from $2^{1}/_{2}$–5 metres (8–16 feet) high, and has a thick stem at the base. The long green stem tapers to a large cluster of grassy, thin leaves that spring from a central tuft of pearl-colored florets.

ISIS AND OSIRIS AND THE TAMARISK TREE

(Tamarix parviflora)

ISIS AND Osiris were born of Nut, goddess of heaven, and Sibou, god of the earth. When Osiris was born, a great voice proclaimed, "The Master of all things has seen the light of day," and cries of joy went up. But this joy turned to tears when the voice told the people that great suffering would befall the child. A man named Pampyles of Thebes, who heard the proclamation, was entrusted by the gods to bring up the child in preparation for his special destiny.

Isis and Osiris were later married and became king and queen. At that time, the Egyptians were cannibalistic, but they also lived on the fruits of the earth. Osiris taught them to recognise the nourishing plants: corn, barley, and grapes. He taught them the principles of agriculture, how to sow and reap corn and barley. Before their eyes, he made wine from

Above: TOMB PAINTING (C.2850 BC) *The departed before Osiris, Isis, and Thoyh*

grapes and beer from barley. He erected temples and taught the people how to worship, and gave them knowledge of life beyond the earth. Osiris was known as Lord of the Green Fields, Master of the Blossoming Vines, and God of the Cornfields.

Isis convinced the Egyptians to abolish cannibalism; she looked after the sick and sent away evil spirits. She showed the people how to grind grain into flour and spin thread with the stalks of flax. While Osiris travelled, taming other peoples, he left Isis in charge of Egypt. He left no land unvisited, spreading civilization far and wide. He is said to have returned to Egypt by a boat whose crew rowed with one oar of cypress and one of juniper.

Set Typhon was Osiris' brother, the third son of Nut. Pretending to welcome Osiris home, Set held a great banquet in his honor. But his plan was to seize the throne from Osiris. At the banquet he displayed a casket he'd had made to Osiris' exact measurements. When its beauty was admired by all the guests, Set joked that whoever it fitted would have it as a gift. Osiris had his turn in the casket, and Set's officers sealed him inside with molten lead. The casket containing Osiris was launched onto the Nile.

Deeply distressed, Isis set off in search of the casket; she was determined not to stop until it was found. She followed trails of sweet clover, for wherever Osiris had passed these little flowers would grow. The casket had been swept down the Nile into the sea and had run aground on the shores of Syria. It came to rest beneath a bush. The bush grew with astonishing rapidity until it became a tamarisk tree, beautiful and tall. It continued to grow until it enveloped the casket. Malcandre, the king of Syria, had the tree chopped down to serve as a pillar to support the roof of his palace.

When Isis discovered Osiris's whereabouts, she implored the king to let her have the casket. She took it back to Egypt and hid it in a lonely spot among reeds and rushes. But the evil Set came across the hidden casket one night. He cut the corpse of his brother into fourteen separate pieces, which he threw in every direction. Once again, Isis set out to search for her husband. One by one, she found thirteen parts. The fourteenth, the phallus, had been devoured by a crab of the Nile. With the god Thoth and her sister Nephthys, Isis embalmed Osiris with a mixture of herbs, grain and incense to keep his body for all eternity, and gave him new life. Osiris was the first Egyptian mummy.

The slender massed branches of the tamarisk *(Tamarix parviflora)* are smothered in feathery, pastel-pink blossoms in spring and summer. It grows along river beds and in marshes in the eastern Mediterranean, and is a symbol of beauty and youth.

ANCIENT CHINESE

The pantheon of immortals believed in by the people of ancient China existed in a beaurocratic system oddly similar to that conducted by the emperors of China.

The gods and goddesses were presided over by the Heavenly Master who reigned over all creation from his palace on the highest level of Heaven. This earliest recognised god, sometimes called Father – Heaven, was said to have created human beings by modelling them in clay. The August Personage ran his court exactly as would any earthly ruler: he could promote, demote or even dismiss gods and goddesses; he also commanded an army, though his consisted of heavenly soldiers who would drive evil spirits from the country. The wife of the Heavenly Master, the Queen Mother Wang, hosted banquets at which guests were served the fruit of immortality – this grew once every three thousand years on peach trees in the imperial orchard.

China's vast history is embroidered with tales of these divinities, and many involve trees and fruit. Religion, agriculture, and the animism that was prevalent among the rural people dictated Chinese myth. Until relatively recent times, many of these beliefs persisted, and offerings were regularly made to favourite deities to ensure fertility and good fortune.

XI WANG MU AND THE FLOWERING PEACH

(Prunus persica)

XI WANG MU, the Queen Mother of the Chinese gods and goddesses, governed the length of mortal life; it was she who could give the blessing of longevity. Her birds were the mythical phoenix and the crane.

The goddess lived in a palace of pure gold ornamented with precious stones, which was surrounded by towering walls. In the gardens within the walls, Xi Wang Mu grew the Peaches of Immortality, each one of which took three thousand years to form and another three thousand years to ripen. When one of these peaches ripened, the goddess celebrated her birth by eating it.

Hou I, known as the heavenly archer who had shot nine of the original ten suns from the sky, built Xi Wang Mu a palace of jade in the Western Heaven. As a reward the goddess gave him an elixir made from the Peaches of Immortality. The magical potion gave off an unearthly light, and Hou I was very tempted to drink it at once. But Xi Wang Mu warned Hou I not to drink any of the potion until he had fasted for one year. Hou I hid the elixir in the roof of his house.

One day, Hou I's wife discovered the hidden elixir. Unaware of its nature, she took a sip from the bottle. As soon as she had swallowed the potion, she felt herself float from the ground. Out through the window she went, rising above the house. Hou I saw her floating in the air and guessed what had happened. Furious, he chased her as far as he could, but she flew faster and higher until she reached the moon. Peaches often feature in Chinese myth and poetry. The flowering peach *(Prunus persica)* is a deciduous, bushy tree that bears delectable stone fruit after blooming with delicate rose-style flowers in the spring.

Above: FLOWERING PEACH *(Prunus persica)*

MAIO SHAN AND THE WHITE LOTUS

(Nymphaea spp.*)*

MAIO SHAN was a princess, the youngest of three sisters, and famous throughout the land for her intelligence, her compassion and her beauty.

One day, she was sitting beneath a tree in the palace gardens. The humming of the cicadas in the branches above her and the warmth of the sun was soporific. Maio Shan daydreamed in bliss surrounded by the scents and colours of a thousand blooms.

She was awakened suddenly when a praying mantis caught a cicada. She climbed the tree to save the cicada, but fell when the mantis went to bite her.

Overcome with compassion, Maio Shan became determined to right the wrongs of the world. She prayed to the Buddha for guidance, and was told of a magical white lotus that grew on the top of Mount Sumeru. If she found the flower and brought it back, her wish would be granted: she would become a Boddhisattva, one who has perfect knowledge.

With her maid, Yung Lien, Maio Shan set off in search of Mount Sumeru and the magical bloom. On the long journey the princess performed many acts of kindness, and

Above: WATER LILY *(Nymphaea)*

was generous and loving to all she met. After seventy days and nights the two weary women had exhausted their supply of food. As they travelled they ate only the berries they gathered from bushes. Finally, after many months of walking, Maio Shan and Yung Lien reached Mount Sumeru. For three days they struggled to reach the summit. At the top they found the Buddha waiting for them, holding a water jug and a perfect white lotus flower.

The Buddha told Maio Shan that she should take the blossom in the jug of water back to the palace. There she should nurture it and devote her life to personal perfection through meditation. Then, one day, the Buddha said, the flower would transform into a willow branch. On this day she would rise to heaven as a Boddhisattva.

Maio Shan returned to the palace, where she obeyed the Buddha's commands. Every day she meditated, denying herself all the luxuries and comforts she had previously known.

After two years, a young boy who lived in the palace, Shan Ying, decided to play a trick on Maio Shan by substituting the lotus blossom in the water jug with a willow branch. But to his consternation, the princess only declared that she had dreamt of a child who had assisted her in achieving perfect knowledge.

One morning, Maio Shan was sitting by a lotus pool staring at the blossoms when she noticed that one of the blooms was growing. Soon it covered the surface of the water. She stepped onto the flower and was gently lifted to heaven; her task of self-perfection was achieved. She was transformed into Guan Yin, goddess of mercy, a guardian angel who would forever more help those in danger.

The lotus flower has appeared as a magic and sacred plant in the mythology of many countries. Its flowers are enjoyed for their shape and fragrance, and the lotus seed is regarded as the food of the fairies. In ancient Greek legend, it was denoted as inducing luxurious dreaminess and a distaste for activity. In ancient Egypt and in China itself, the lotus flower was a water lily (*Nymphaea* spp.), which symbolized death, rebirth, and divination.

Most water lilies have a rich perfume, and are found in a number of shades, including red, white, gold, and pink. They bloom through the warm weather, with both flowers and leaves floating on top of the water.

THE WILLOW PATTERN STORY AND THE WEEPING WILLOW

(Salix babylonica)

IN DAYS long ago, when China was ruled by emperors, there lived by a river a rich mandarin, T'so Ling, who had a beautiful daughter, Koong-se. Although they possessed everything the heart could desire, these two were not happy.

T'so Ling was unhappy because he had a guilty conscience; he had accepted bribes in the days he had served the Emperor. He hired a clerk called Chang to destroy all the records of his dishonesty. Then Koong-se fell in love with Chang and was unhappy too, because she knew that they could never be together: she was the daughter of a wealthy mandarin, and Chang was but a poor clerk. Chang returned her love, and each day when he had finished his work he would write her a love poem.

Koong-se had a young handmaiden, the wife of the gardener who tended the trees and flowers around the house. There were persimmon, peach, and almond trees, and camellias, purple irises and deep-red peonies. The kind handmaiden helped the two lovers meet secretly in the garden.

One evening, the mandarin discovered Chang and Koong-se together. He banished Chang from his house, and built a set of rooms over the river in which to keep Koong-se. Chang could not row to the house without being visible; and if he tried to cross the bridge that spanned the river where a weeping willow grew, he would be seen at once.

68

The beautiful blue and white china tells the charming willow pattern story

Soon afterwards, T'so Ling told Koong-se she was to marry a wealthy widower, the Ta-jin, a friend of his, when the peach tree blossomed in the spring. Koong-se pined for Chang, and watched in despair as buds grew on the peach tree.

One afternoon, Koong-se found a coconut shell floating on the river; in it was a message from Chang. The message declared Chang's love for her, and said that he would destroy himself when she married the rich widower. She placed a message in the coconut pleading with Chang to rescue her, and floated it back down the river; but she heard no reply.

In time, the peach-tree buds were about to burst into blossom, and the wealthy widower, the great lord Ta-jin, arrived. As was the custom, T'so Ling entertained him, and the wine flowed in abundance. Deep in the shadow of a cypress tree, a stranger waited until both servants and masters were sleeping in a drunken stupor, and then Chang, for it was he, crept to Koong-se's rooms.

Together the lovers fled, with a box of jewels that the Ta-jin had given Koong-se, but just as they crossed the bridge T'so Ling stirred and saw them. He gave chase, hunting whip in hand, but could not catch them. He had to return and tell the Ta-jin, who was furious.

The lovers hid not far from the mandarin's house in the home of the gardener and his wife. Here they were married, and they ventured out only after nightfall to avoid discovery. They planned that the gardener would not return home from T'so Ling's at his usual time if suspicion had fallen on the house in which they were living.

One evening the gardener failed to return home, and Koong-se trembled in fear, for she knew something was wrong. Soldiers came to the house, but the gardener's wife waylaid them and the lovers hid. Chang escaped through a window, and then came back to collect Koong-se in a boat; together they were carried away on the river. For several days they sailed until they came upon an uninhabited island. Here they settled and prospered, sowing seed, planting trees and growing fruit.

Chang became a well-known agriculturalist, and eventually the Ta-jin, now an old man, heard of him and determined to wreak his revenge. He gathered some soldiers and attacked the island, killing Chang with his sword. Koong-se, in horror, ran to their home and set it on fire, perishing in its midst.

The gods looked down from above and cursed the Ta-jin for his cruelty; soon after, he died alone. They then rewarded the constancy and undying love of Chang and Koong-se by transforming their spirits into two immortal doves, which would live forever in the branches of the weeping willow tree.

The willow tree is sacred to many peoples, and is known in myth to be a tree of enchantment, divination and prophecy. The weeping willow *(Salix babylonica)* is Chinese in origin, and is found near rivers and streams. It is a wide-crowned tree with bending branches that touch the ground, hence its name. The Chinese willow pattern is produced in blue on white china and has been a favourite since its introduction to England in 1780.

EARLY CHRISTIAN

It could be said that some of the most recent mythology is found within Christianity. The gods and goddesses of ancient Greece and Rome were forgotten once Jesus Christ was accepted, and the Christian religion prevailed. The Old Testament creation story is understood to be an account of the beginning of history. The Christian-based nature of many societies indicates that religion and magic still figure in people's everyday lives and dreams.

A number of Christian saints are legendary characters whose stories involve plants. When St. Dorothy, for example, was being led to her execution because she would not be converted from Christianity, a scornful lawyer asked her to send him some fruit and flowers from heaven when she got there. Immediately, a small child appeared bearing roses and apples; the lawyer was converted on the spot.

Perhaps the best known Christian story of fruit and trees is that of Adam and Eve. The Bible says that Adam, created by God out of the dust of the earth, and Eve, who was made from one of Adam's ribs, lived innocently in the Garden of Eden. Then Eve was tempted by Satan, disguised as a serpent, to eat the forbidden fruit, the apples of the Tree of Knowledge. She convinced Adam to eat the fruit as well. As punishment, an angel drove them from the Garden, and God declared that Adam must earn his bread "in the sweat of thy face" and that Eve must bear children "in sorrow". A piece of apple is said to have stuck in Adam's throat, and hence, according to this, males have Adam's apples.

> *And out of the ground made the Lord God to grow every tree that is*
> *pleasant to the sight, and good for food; the tree of life also in the midst*
> *of the garden, and the tree of knowledge of good and evil*
>
> Genesis 2 v. 9

The tree of life was believed to preside over immortality, and the tree of knowledge over wisdom. "Eating from the tree of knowledge" nowadays implies that knowledge can only be acquired with the high price of loss of innocence.

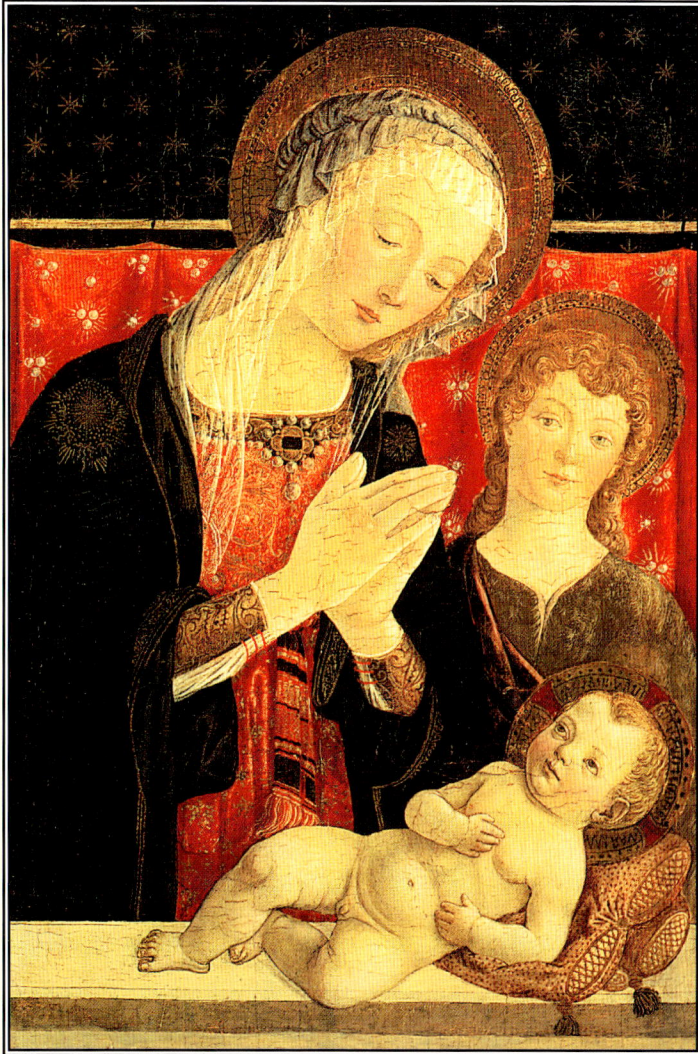

Madonna and Child with St. John the Baptist

CHRIST
AND
THE PASSION FLOWER
(Passiflora incarnata)

THE LEGEND of the passion flower began when Spanish settlers went to South America in the 16th century. Devout Christians from Spain saw for the first time the native climbing plant *Passiflora incarnata* with its complex design and arresting flowers of crimson, blue, pink, yellow or pale lime green.

On closely examining the flower, the pious Spaniards found that its intricate formation lent itself to religious association. In the plant's structure and the numerical arrangement of its components, many symbols of Christ's Crucifixion and resurrection were found. The blooms all have the same distinctive composition: the five antlers, comparable to Christ's five wounds; an ovary stem, comparable to the pillar of the cross; three strong stamens, like hammers for the nailing; a prominent fringed middle, which could represent the crown of thorns; and the calyx, which became a symbol of Christ's halo.

The flower drops and falls after three days, recalling the three days and nights Christ spent "in the heart of the earth", before he was resurrected.

Above: PASSION FLOWER *(Passiflora incarnata)*

THE YOUNG JESUS AND THE DATE PALM

(Phoenix dactylifera)

W HEN JESUS was a child He performed a number of miracles. One legend tells of the time when the Holy Family were fleeing in fear from King Herod, who'd ordered his soldiers to find and kill Jesus.

On the way to Egypt, Jesus and his parents were surrounded by gambolling lions and leopards. Mary was afraid of the huge animals but Jesus assured her they were harmless. Indeed, the animals protected them and worshipped Jesus by bowing their heads.

The family stopped to rest, hungry and tired, beneath a tall palm tree that was heavy with ripe dates. Mary longed for the fruit, but Joseph was unable to reach them for her.

Jesus is said to have commanded the palm to bow down. It bent over, its fronds reaching Mary's feet, and offered its fruit to the hungry family. They ate their fill of the sweet, rich dates and the tree remained bowed submissively until Jesus ordered it to stand straight again.

The date palm (*Phoenix dactylifera*) is found on the desert fringe that runs from North Africa through the Middle East, and has been used for food and shelter since time immemorial. The tree can survive with little water, and the fruit is orange-red and sweet.

Above: DATE PALM *(Phoenix dactylifera)*

JOSEPH OF ARIMATHEA AND THE GLASTONBURY THORN

(*Crataegus monogyna* or *C. oxyacantha*)

From our old books I know
That Joseph came of old to Glastonbury
LORD TENNYSON

I
N ABOUT the year 60 A.D., Joseph of Arimathea went from Palestine to Britain with twelve companions to preach the Gospel. A British chief, Arvirigus, allowed him to settle on the Isle of Glastonbury – the "Glass Island", which was once surrounded by smooth, clear lakes. Here legend and history merge: Glastonbury is historically part of the mysterious Isle of Avalon – the Isle of Apples – whose heart was formed by a group of orchard hills. The island also features in the legends of King Arthur (see the next section in this book).

A member of the Jewish senate, Joseph became a secret disciple of Christ. After the Crucifixion, Christ's body was laid in the tomb previously prepared for Joseph. Joseph then left Jerusalem and journeyed to Britain with the Holy Grail. He and his brethren built a church of wattle and daub, the first place in Britain in which the name of Christ was taught. Pilgrims journeyed from far places to worship there.

Right: HAWTHORN *(Crataegus monogyne)*

Chroniclers say that when Joseph came to Glastonbury with his followers he rested on Weary-all Hill. As he sat down he stuck his staff into the ground, whereupon it sprouted into a thorn tree, immediately coming into bud. On every Christmas Day thereafter, snow-white blossoms appeared on the thorn tree grown from the great man's staff; and, it is said, the tree flowered again in May each year. Joseph's miraculous thorn flourished on the hill for centuries before it was mutilated by Puritans.

Descendants of the Holy Thorn continue to grow. There is now a fine thorn tree in the grounds of the Abbey ruins, and another in St. John's churchyard in Glastonbury. From the latter, following an ancient custom, sprigs were cut at Christmas time and sent to the monarch.

There is no confirmation as to which species of thorn, or hawthorn, made Joseph's staff. The hawthorn growing wild on hillsides, in ravines, and in hedges in the northern Mediterranean *(Crataegus oxycantha)* was believed to grow in the south also, but botanists assert that the latter variety is the hawthorn *C. monogyna,* which is considered by some researchers to be the Glastonbury Thorn. *Crataegus monogyna* is the hawthorn "whitethorn", or "may", that is seen in hedges and is self-sown in the wild.

Hawthorn's botanical name of *Crataegus* is derived from the Greek word *kratos,* meaning strength, which represents the hardness of the wood. Hawthorn was used to make small articles; the root-wood was particularly good for carving into boxes and combs. There are legends of the hawthorn's magical qualities, and at one time the branches were a Turkish symbol of love.

ST JOHN
AND THE CAROB TREE

(Ceratonia siliqua)

IT IS a belief that the carob tree's ripe bean pods are the "locusts" that sustained St. John the Baptist during his wanderings in the wilderness. The carob pods have also been referred to as "locust pods" and "St. John's Bread". They feature in the biblical Parable of the Prodigal Son who, before leaving home, asked his father for his inheritance which he consequently squandered on riotous living. When the son had no money or food left, he hired himself out as a keeper of swine; he was so hungry he longed to eat the carob husks that were fed to the animals.

Carob husks have been widely used since biblical times as sustenance for both humans and domestic animals. People in the Middle East still regard them as a nourishing food. Beans from the carob tree *(Ceratonia siliqua)* are a source of energy, caffeine free and low in fat; they would certainly have helped St. John survive in a hostile environment. The sweet taste of carob is similar to that of cocoa and chocolate, without any dietary drawbacks in its composition. Whole dried pods can be chewed as they are, but ground carob is more practical to use and is easily available. A syrup is also processed from carob, called "dibs" in the Middle East. Historically, the seeds of the carob are said to have been the jeweller's original carat weight.

Above: CAROB TREE *(Ceratonia siliqua)*

79

THE LEGEND OF THE CROSS

ACCORDING TO legend, the dogwood tree once grew straight and tall. But this was so only until a dogwood was used to make the cross on which Jesus was crucified. As a memorial to the event, dogwoods have never again grown large enough to be used for this purpose.

In the spring, when the dogwood blooms, the four-petal arrangement of its flowers is reminiscent of the cross. Each white petal has an indentation on its outer edge –- a symbol of the nail marks on the Saviour's hands. Then, in the autumn, the leaves of the dogwood turn a fiery red to commemorate the blood of Jesus with which human salvation was secured.

The dogwood (*Cornus* spp.) is also known as redtwig or clusterberry. Dogwoods are all deciduous trees; there are over a hundred species, each exquisite in their bloomings of white, pink or red flowers in the spring. In the autumn dogwoods produce a spectacular display of clustered fruit.

Above: KOUSA DOGWOOD *(Cornus kousa)*

ST. JOHN THE BAPTIST AND ST. JOHN'S WORT

(Hypericum perforatum)

ST. JOHN the Baptist was a spiritual visionary and a celibate. The prophets of old had written that he was to be the messenger who would prepare the way for Jesus, the Son of God. John preached to the people of Judea and Jerusalem; they were all baptized by him in the river of Jordan and confessed to their sins.

When Jesus came from Nazareth to be baptized, John said humbly that he could only baptize with water, but that God would baptize Him with the Holy Ghost. As Jesus stepped out of the water, the heavens opened, and the Spirit descended upon Him like a dove. Then Jesus went forth, after overcoming the Temptation in the Wilderness, and began preaching the gospel of the kingdom of God.

Meanwhile, Herod Antipas, governor of Galilee and Peraea, had imprisoned John the Baptist, for his wife Herodias' sake. She had formerly been married to Herod's brother Philip and John had said to Herod, "It is not lawful for thee to have thy brother's wife" (Mark 6 v. 18). Herodias demanded that John be killed at once; but Herod forbade it, as he knew John was a just man to whom he had listened gladly. Herod was also frightened of the multitude who believed in the words of John.

When his birthday came, Herod gave a large banquet, inviting all the high officials and land owners of Galilee. During the celebrations, the beautiful young daughter of Herodias, Salome, danced. She abandoned herself to the rhythmic movements of the evocative dance. All who watched were bewitched, especially Herod, who told her that she could have whatever reward she asked, even if that were half his kingdom. Youthful Salome went to her mother, saying, "What shall I ask?"

Herodias answered, "The head of John the Baptist" (Mark 6 v. 24). Herod was saddened by Salome's request that the Baptist's head be severed and given to her "in a charger" (on a plate). Nevertheless, as Herod had given the oath before his guests he knew he must keep it. He sent forth an executioner, commanding him to behead John in prison. Once this was done, the executioner brought John's head –

in a charger and gave it to the damsel: and the damsel gave it to her mother Mark 6 v. 28

Hypericum is a rounded, bushy plant with golden, five-petalled blossoms. When the starry blossoms are crushed, they expel a glowing, red pigment, hypericine, which was thought to signify the blood of the Baptist when he was beheaded. Hypericum was therefore assigned to St. John. The flowers appear in summer through to mid-autumn in cool climates. The shrub is in full bloom on 24 June each year, so this date became St. John's "Saint's Day". The shrub was known thereafter as St. John's Wort.

John The Baptist preaching

ARTHURIAN

King Arthur of the Round Table was probably based on an historical figure who lived during the turbulent years of the 6th century A.D. This chieftain's life, now in the hinterland of history, merged into myth and the romance of the Age of Chivalry. Geoffrey Chaucer, Sir Thomas Mallory, John Masefield, and Alfred, Lord Tennyson are just a few of the noted men of letters whose imaginations were fired by the legends of this leader of Christianity during England's Dark Ages. Tales of Arthur's life: his birth, boyhood, ascent to kingship, and victorious battles have held people's fascination for centuries.

Under the guidance of the magician Merlin, Arthur became King of England at the age of fifteen. As King he led the knights of the Round Table at Camelot, and many stories tell of their battles and their loves. But the focus of most of the legends is the search for the Holy Grail.

Tales of Arthur's magical jewelled sword, Excalibur, of the glamour of his Court at "many-tower'd" Camelot, and of the noble quests undertaken by his knights are all woven into inspired prose-narrative and poetry. Also intrinsic to the legend of Arthur is the love story between Guinevere, Arthur's queen and Lancelot, a knight of the Round Table.

The tales of King Arthur and his knights are both great and romantic; and though they do reflect the violence and cruelty of the time, they demonstrate the virtues of gallantry and chivalry. The stories are made even more enchanting by magic, wizards, herb decoctions and potions. Two of the most mysterious characters from these romances are the wise magician, Merlin, and the sorceress, Morgan-le-Fay. The following legends tell of their use of herbs and other plants to control their world.

Right: A knight of the round table in King Arthur's wood

MERLIN AND THE OAK TREE
(Quercus robur)

AND MISTLETOE
(Viscum album)

"Sir," said Merlin to King Uther
I know all your heart every deal. So ye will be sworn
unto me as ye be a true king anointed, to fulfil my
desire, ye shall have your desire.

SIR THOMAS MALLORY
Le Morte d'Arthur

MERLIN, the all-knowing wise man of Britain, was a wizard. Child of a princess and an evil spirit who seduced her, Merlin was a supernatural being. He could change himself into various forms, had foreknowledge, and was a specialist at casting spells.

Merlin connived with King Uther Pendragon, who had fallen in love with Igraine, the Duke of Tintagel's wife. When the Duke was away fighting a battle, Merlin helped Uther gain access to Igraine. Tintagel Castle was impregnable, so Merlin disguised Uther as the duke and, with the help of magic, the royal imposter gained entry to the castle. Finding Igraine's chamber, Uther entered. Igraine believed that her husband had returned, and Arthur was conceived that night.

When news of the duke's death was brought to the duchess the next day, she guessed what had occurred. Uther wasted no time in making Igraine his queen. When Arthur was born, Merlin came to take him away: this was the reward Uther had promised when the wizard aided his entry into Tintagel Castle. Merlin handed the baby to Sir Ector and his wife to bring up under his own supervision. The wizard was Arthur's guide and mentor, and groomed the boy for the great position that awaited him.

Right: The wizard Merlin falls victim to his own magical crafts when turned upon by his mistress, Viviane

I

II

Viscum
Viscus quercinus

1. 2. *Beer*
3. 5. *Blatt*

Eichen-Mistell

Merlin's eyes were penetrating, his personality dynamic. He had a long, thick beard, wore a full-length robe and carried a wizard's wand. He admired "fair damosels", in particular, the Lady of the Lake, Viviane (or Nimiane or Nimue). She became his mistress, and he was so enthralled by her that he rarely left her side. Viviane knew many magic arts, but Merlin knew more. They went from Camelot on a journey together, and she enchanted him into revealing to her his sorcery's secret arts. When they were sitting in a forest, she seized the opportunity to be rid of her tiresome lover. Using one of Merlin's most powerful spells, she imprisoned the wretched wizard in an oak tree from which he would never be able to free himself, despite his magical craft.

Certain trees in every country are believed to be the dwelling places of fairies or tree spirits and are known as fairy trees. These trees also have beneficial qualities for human use. In fable, the oak tree *(Quercus robur)* is chief among fairy trees. Oaks have also been considered the most sacred of trees owing to their association with Druid worship and the parasite, mistletoe, which gains its extra healing potency from its host, the oak.

The oak's branches, which are massive and spread widely with a downward sweep, produce a dome-like mass. The flowers, appearing in spring to summer, are tiny, and are followed by the acorn-fruit. Oak trees are deciduous, and can live for hundreds of years. It is said that when an oak is cut down, an oak coppice can spring from the roots.

This majestic tree has had great symbolic, religious, practical, and magical importance in Europe since time immemorial. It has provided wood for constructing buildings, ships, tools, and fine furniture. The bark, which was formerly used for tanning leather and making dyes, provides valuable medicine used in herbal therapy and homeopathy. The dried bark has astringent, anti-inflammatory, and antiseptic properties. Roasted acorns are known as a coffee substitute.

Mistletoe *(Viscum album)* is a healing plant that is a bushy parasite. It grows on the bark of several trees, but when growing on an oak tree it has special virtues. The ancient Druids collected mistletoe, with golden sickles, from oak trees only, as they knew this mistletoe had the greatest power for use in their rites. They wore white robes to harvest the plant, before handing it to a white-clad Druid waiting with a spotless cloth. The mistletoe was then borne away by white oxen.

Left: Mistletoe *(Viscum album)*

MORGAN–LE–FAY

ONE OF THE MOST enigmatic beings close to King Arthur was Morgan-le-Fay, his fairy half-sister.

Morgan, also known as Morgaine and Morgana, was schooled on the mysterious island of Avalon, where she was initiated into the secret arts of preparing magical potions from herbs and in the casting of spells.

> *And the third sister Morgan-le-Fay was*
> *put to school in a nunnery, and there she*
> *learned so much that she was a great*
> *clerk of necromancy …*
>
> SIR THOMAS MALLORY
> *Le Morte d'Arthur*

It is said in some legends that when Morgan came to Camelot from Avalon she felt a distrust of Arthur's wife, the Queen Guinevere. The King and Queen longed for a son, but Morgan was determined to prevent the queen from conceiving. The young sorceress put a royal servant-woman under a spell. She instructed the woman in the preparation of a decoction from the active parts of certain herbs collected at their most potent times.

Roots of hellebore, lovage and sweet flag were simmered and strained, then mixed with juices from the leaves of vervain, pennyroyal, rue and wood-sorrel. Bitter, unpleasant tastes were effectively disguised by stirring honey and sweet wine into the brew. This drink, poured into a silver goblet and then carried to the unsuspecting queen each morning, ensured that Guinevere's monthly periods continued with regularity.

Right: The young sorceress, Morgan-le-Fay practised the secret art of preparing magical potions from herbs

Some decades later King Arthur fell in battle defending his throne. His knights had either also fallen in the field, or made their way to a monastery to join the Brotherhood. Guinevere fled to a nunnery. Arthur's fabled kingdom vanished, and Camelot was no more.

Morgan of the Fairies returned to the Isle of Avalon, which at that time was veiled in silver mists, existing in another dimension—initiates alone knew how to find their way there.

Deep-meadow's happy, fair with orchard-lawns
And bowery hollows crown'd with summer sea …

ALFRED, LORD TENNYSON
Morte d'Arthur

The dying King Arthur was rowed to Avalon in a black-draped barge, attended by three queens, one of whom was Morgan. By now she had been married for a time to King Uriens of the land of Gore. Arthur was healed of his wounds, and lived with other great heroes on this mystical island. He is ready to return when his countryfolk need him:

So Arthur passed, but country-folk believe
He will return, to triumph, and achieve;
Men watch for him on each Midsummer Eve.

JOHN MASEFIELD
Gwenivere Tells

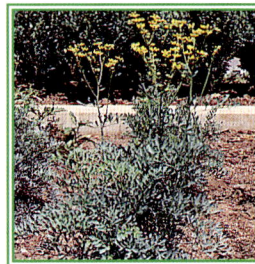

From left: The herbs lovage, pennyroyal and rue were used in Morgan-le-Fay's magical decoctions

In old dayes of the King Artour
Of which that Bretons speken great honour,
All was this land fulfilled of faeries;
The elf-quene with hire jolie company
Daunced full of te in many a grene mede;
This was the old opinion as I rede,
I speke of many hundred yeres agoe,
But now can no man see non elves mo.

CHAUCER 1340 – 1400

THE ABORIGINAL DREAMTIME

The myths and legends of the Australian Aborigines tell of the ancient Dreamtime, the time when the world was created.

Stories vary from tribe to tribe, but most believe that in the beginning the earth was flat and uninhabited. Then from out of the plains rose giant creatures, who were at the same time human and non-human. They roamed the country creating mountain ranges, rivers, billabongs and rock formations; they established the life patterns that are still, in some areas, followed today. When the tasks of creation were done, the ancestors sank back into the earth, and the Dreamtime came to an end. But the Dreaming never ended. It was and is everywhere, its creative power drawn on by the Aboriginal people during their songs and ceremonies.

Many legends are connected with plants, berries and seeds, as the gathering of food was an important part of life. While few stories mention the beauty of flowers, there are some stories in which flowering plants are personified.

THE 'FIRE' TREE
(*Xanthorrhea* spp)

THERE ARE a number of Aboriginal myths featuring the origin of fire. These myths vary from tribe to tribe. One tells of a young man who set out on a journey to find the one tribe in the Dreamtime who knew how fire was made.

For a long time he walked day and night across the land. Occasionally he came upon other tribes, but none of them knew how fire was made or even what it was. At last the young man came to a vast mountain range, where he found some children playing. He vowed that if the tribe who knew how to make fire did not live on this mountain, he would turn for home.

He watched the children for a while, and noticed that they were healthier and stronger that those of his own tribe. Perhaps they did belong to the tribe who knew how to make fire? As evening grew, the children began to climb to the top of the mountain and the young man followed them. He climbed a tree so that no one would see him, and from his perch he could see the glow of a bright fire. Now he needed a way to take the precious fire back to his people.

Nearby a grass tree was growing, and he chopped it down to its roots and took out the core. He intended to take a burning stick of fire from the tribe's fire and put it inside the grass tree, so that he could carry it home.

The young man waited until everybody in the camp was asleep, and then made his way to the fire. He took a lighted stick from the fire and put it into the core of the grass tree. Then he ran down the mountain. On the way to his home, he gave fire to the many tribes that he encountered. From that time, whenever fire was needed, the Aborigines took a flower stem of the grass tree and rubbed it vigorously with a piece of harder wood to make fire for cooking, warmth and protection.

Above: GRASS TREE *(Xanthorrhea)*

THE GIFT OF FLOWERS

THE GREAT Spirit, Baiame, once lived on earth and made his home in a mountain. He talked with the animals and the men and women whom he had created, and looked with pleasure on the flowers that bloomed around his home. One day, he announced to all around him that it was time for him to leave. "While the earth was young you needed me, but now you are fully grown. It is better that you live by yourselves."

The people were sad and afraid, but Baiame told them not to be fearful. He would be near them, and he would return in the form of a man when they needed him.

The animals wandered away, but the men and women stayed, loath to leave the delightful, scented flowers around the mountain where Baiame had lived. At night they lay on the many-hued carpet and stared up at the Milky Way in search of the Great Spirit.

One morning, something was wrong. A woman cried out, "The flowers are gone!" The flowers had not understood Baiame's words; they had mourned for the Father Spirit, and one by one they had died. Now the earth was bare of plants and flowers, and the bees also began to die.

"Now we shall have no honey!" the women cried in despair. Then, around them, trees began to rise from the ground, and down their trunks flowed clear liquid that the people had never seen before. The liquid tasted good, and now the people knew that Baiame still loved them.

For many years, though, the flowers did not grow. Only the story of the Death of the Flowers remained, and Baiame felt sorry for his people. He put into their minds a great longing, and gradually some of the men travelled to the place where the flowers had once grown. Baiame was there, and he gathered the people to him and lifted them up to the sky. There he set them on a cloud and showed them a glowing carpet of flowers, which stretched as far as they could see. "Gather armfuls of them now and take them back to earth with you. They will gladden your hearts for ever."

Baiame set the men gently back on earth, and they raced back to their tribes, scattering flowers as they ran. Never again will the earth be without flowers while the Great Spirit watches over his people.

WAMILI AND THE WARATAH
(Telopea speciosissima)

L̲ong ago in the Dreamtime, there lived a skilled hunter, Wamili, who dwelt with his people in the bountiful eucalyptus forests. He could track any animal with his keen eyesight and sure instinct, and then aim truly with his spear at bounding kangaroos, running emus, and swift small animals. Wamili was more gifted a marksman than all the other hunters, so gifted that he alone was able to keep his people supplied with nourishment.

Wamili did not care for meat, however. He preferred the sweet nectar of the waratah flowers, and whenever possible he would seek them out and drink his fill. At that time, the waratah resembled a daisy, although it produced honeyed nectar during the summer.

Life went on like this for many seasons, until one day when Wamili and the other men were away from the camp hunting. Wamili was treading softly and watching the ground, when suddenly heavy, black clouds darkened the sky, thunder filled the air, and flashes of terrible lightning struck the ground close to the men.

As Wamili and the others ran for shelter, a lightning dart struck Wamili as accurately as his own spear had found its mark while hunting. He fell to the ground as if dead. His friends desperately tried to revive him, and eventually he regained consciousness.

Above: Waratah *(Telopea speciosissima)*

But a catastrophe had occurred, for the streak of lightning had blinded Wamili.

The great hunter could no longer track the animals or aim with his spear. Wamili was sad and weak after his ordeal, and he sought the sweet nectar of the waratah flowers to give him strength. He searched for his favourite food, but could only feel for the blooms with his hands; nor could he tell the difference between honeyed flowers and those that were poisonous and bitter.

One day, Wamili's wife, feeling sorry for her beloved husband, decided to seek help from the little mountain spirits, the Kwinnies, who lived in the bush. She looked everywhere for them, calling from daybreak to sunset. Then, unexpectedly, she stumbled upon a group of the little spirits. She related the tale of her husband's misfortune, and explained that he had been a great and unselfish hunter of food. She also told them that he enjoyed the waratah nectar far more than meat, and that, because of his blindness, he could no longer find the flowers.

The Kwinnies listened kindly, and were sympathetic. They said they would lengthen the stalk of the waratah making it easier to reach, and change the shape of the blossom so it would feel like no other flower. Wamili's wife thanked the Kwinnies, and hurried home to her husband with a light heart.

Overnight the Kwinnies did as they had promised. They changed the waratah into a splendid red bloom with an upstanding rounded head encircled by frills of petals. It was different in shape and texture from all other flowers.

Wamili was now able to distinguish the waratahs with his hands, and it was with gratitude that he now drank their nectar.

The impressive waratah blooms in the Australian bush from late spring to summer in the mountainous regions of eastern Australia. It is a tall, slender shrub with leathery, lobed leaves and large, crimson flowers which attract honey eating birds and native bees.

PURLIMIL AND BOROLA AND THE "FLOWERS OF BLOOD"— STURT'S DESERT PEA

(Clianthus formosus)

I N THE HEART of Australia, the vast expanse of earth is burnt to a glowing red under the blazing sun. The high blue sky sometimes fades to the colour of milky opals in the intense heat. Here, in the middle of the continent, a pretty Aboriginal girl, Purlimil, lived with her people. Purlimil fell in love with Borola, a gentle and worthy young man, and they wished to marry. However, all marriages were arranged by the Elders, who had already decided that Purlimil should marry Tirlta.

A much older man, Tirlta was both irritable and crusty. Purlimil objected to the match, and told the Elders she loved Borola; but they were unmoved, and insisted she should be Tirlta's wife.

Above: STURT'S DESERT PEA *(Clianthus formosus)*

Borola and Purlimil were both very upset, and together wondered what to do. Borola told Purlimil their only hope was to run far away to another place.

One night, after a fiery sunset, when the sky had turned indigo and the diamond-bright stars shone, the lovers quietly and swiftly escaped from the camp. They journeyed for several days and nights under the hot sun, until they came to a shimmering blue lake. On its shores lived some of Borola's relatives, who welcomed the young couple to their camp. Borola and Purlimil were married, and lived in great happiness with these people.

Back at the camp from where the lovers had come, Tirlta was still furious that his intended wife had fled from him, and anger smouldered in his heart. One day he heard from some hunters of the whereabouts of the pair, and so he planned his revenge. He gathered some warriors around him and they set out for the lakeside camp. At night, Tirlta and his men cruelly assaulted the sleeping lakeside people, and all were killed, including Purlimil and Borola.

When the warriors left, the ground was stained with the blood of the peaceful lake community. The ancestor spirits watching from above were so grieved at the merciless killing that they cried for days. Their tears fell into the surrounding lakes, turning the waters salty.

At last Tirlta had completed his revenge, but the massacre was not enough for him; he wanted to return to the area so that he could exult over the dead bodies of his victims. A few months later, with this thought in mind, he journeyed to the lakeside again. When he arrived he looked with amazement at the sight before him: the earth was covered with a wide carpet of dazzling scarlet flowers. The ancestor spirits, in their sympathy and distress for the good lake people, had caused the flowers to grow from their blood in memory of their kindly natures. In the centre of each flower was a shining black circle. To Tirlta, each of these black circles resembled an eye. Then Tirlta's instincts told him what had happened, and he realized that the eyes of the lakeside people were watching him.

He became afraid and began to run away. The spirits overhead saw this, and sent just punishment for his evil deeds by killing him with a spirit spear. As he fell dead, Tirlta was changed into a little stone just like all the other stones on the ground.

The inland lakes of Australia still hold the salty tears of the ancestor spirits and, in the continent's heart, beautiful "Flowers of Blood", now called Sturt's Desert Pea, bloom in profusion in remembrance of Purlimil and Borola.

NATIVE AMERICAN

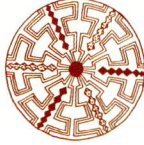

The mythology of the native people of North America is similar among the many different tribes despite their physical distance from one another. Traditions and rituals vary, but all the tribes share a mystical perception of nature, and myths and legends are based on a common belief system regarding the creation of the universe. The earth is seen as the great mother; and the woods, forests, plains, rivers and sky are thought to be represented by spirits.

Native Americans are very knowledgeable about plants and their properties, often using them in medicines and in ceremonies. Many legends tell how a particular plant came into being, and how its spirit could be kept contended. Some plants were thought to have magical powers and were considered sacred. The thornapple, for example, was regarded as magical among many tribes, especially in the California region. For the Navajo, it had great power, and collecting the holy plant was a ritual activity. If a person took too much of the plant and it died, the leaves collected were rendered useless.

Other stories relate how tribes came into being because of plants. A Sioux legend tells that in the beginning, the Sioux people lived far underground in a dark, dank village on the shores of a huge lake. One day, some members of the tribe found that the roots of a huge grape vine *(Vitis vinifera)* had penetrated their land. They climbed the plant to see what the upper world was like. They emerged into bright sunlight to find an abundance of plants growing and animals roaming. Full of excitement, they gathered together the whole tribe to climb the roots of the vine, and from that time forth the Sioux lived in the light and fertility of the upper world.

The more modern myths seem to have been influenced by the coming of the Europeans, but they still retain the archetypes and symbols unique to the native people of North America.

A typical encampment on Lake Huron. Native American tribes considered plants sacred and believed they were represented by spirits

HIAWATHA AND CORN

(Zea mays)

…Till at length a small green feather
From the earth shot slowly upward,
Then another and another,
And before the Summer ended
Stood the maize in all its beauty,
With its shining robes about it,
And its long, soft, yellow tresses:
And in rapture Hiawatha
Cried aloud, "It is Mondamon!
Yes, the friend of man, Mondamin!"

LONGFELLOW
The Song of Hiawatha

HIAWATHA, the 16th century Onondago chief credited with the organisation of the Five Nations, assumed legendary status among the native peoples of North America. He was said to have been a person of divine or miraculous birth sent to earth to teach the Native Americans peace, navigation, medicine and agriculture (especially the cultivation of corn or maize).

The corn plant is tall. Round, golden kernels of corn *(Zea mays)* are formed on an ear, or "cob", which is surrounded by a green husk. Corn is the only cereal known to have originated in the Americas. Tiny husks of wild corn were found by the natives of South America thousands of years ago. Pictures of the wild grass from which corn descends have been found in pre-Inca tombs, which suggests that the Peruvian Indians first cultivated corn in the Andes. Later, this primitive corn was taken north, where it was hybridized with another type of corn in Central America. When the early English settlers arrived in North America, the Native Americans showed them how to plant and use corn.

Right: CORN *(Zea mays)*

104

Graminaceæ

This story from the Huichol people in the north-east of the Rio Grande emphasizes the importance of corn to the Native Americans.

There was once a man who chopped down trees as he prepared his land to plant his corn. Each morning, he awoke to find that the trees had grown again. By the fifth day, full of frustration, he determined to find out what was happening. He stayed up all night and watched. And then he saw a fantastic sight.

An old woman rose from the ground in the clearing he had made. She wielded a stick, pointing it first south, then north, then west, and east; finally she moved the stick up and down. All the trees the man had felled instantly stood up again and lived.

He summoned up enough courage to approach the old woman. When he complained about her actions, she told him that in five days a great flood would arise, along with a cold, bitter wind. She advised the man to make from the wood of a fig tree a box he could fit into. With him he should take five grains of each color of corn, some fire, and five squash stems to burn. He should also take a black female dog.

The man obeyed these instructions, and on the fifth day all was prepared. He climbed into the box, and the old woman fitted the lid carefully. She then perched on top with a parrot and a macaw on each shoulder. The rain began, and the box drifted to all corners of the earth, finally coming to rest on a mountain top.

When the man emerged from the wooden box the earth was covered in water. The old woman's two birds began to create rivers and oceans, and soon the water subsided. When the land was dry, the Earth Mother, for that is who the old woman was, planted grasses and trees.

Once again the man turned to clearing land for his harvest, while the black dog remained in their cave. Each evening, he returned to find corn cakes prepared for him. After five days he decided to hide in the bushes and watch the camp. He saw the dog take off her skin and become a young woman. She ground the corn and prepared the food. The man crept up and flung the dog skin into the fire. The woman began to whine like a dog. Gently, the man bathed her with water mixed with ground corn, and she remained human. The man and woman had many children and with them they began the human race. They planted corn and lived happily for many years.

PICTURE CREDITS

AKG LONDON

Back cover & p. 42: The Sea Voyage of Dionysus, Greek vase painting, Exekias (active c.550-510 BC in Athens)

p. 17: The Birth of Venus, Sandro Botticelli, (1445-1510), Florence, Galleria degli Uffizi

p. 35: Minerva taming the Centaur, Sandro Botticelli, (1445-1510), Florence, Galleria degli Uffizi

p. 59: Queen Nefertari sacrificing two vases to the Goddess Hathor, C19th Dynasty Egyptian painting from grave of Queen Nefertari

p. 75: Date Palm (Phoenix dactylifera), colour lithograph from a series of illustrations "The most important foreign cultivated plants", Leipzig 1899

p. 81: Christ on the Cross/Dream of Nebukadnezzar, Westphalia, c. 1360

p. 93: Morgan le Fay showing King Arthur Guinevere's infidelity with Lancelot, book illumination, French, 15th Century, from Le livre de Lancelot du lac

AUSTRALIAN PICTURE LIBRARY/E.T. ARCHIVE

p. 2 & p. 52: Roman fresco of Goddess Flora or Spring from Stabia near Naples Italy destroyed by Vesuvius eruption, Archaeological Museum Naples

p. 21: Myrtaceae myrtle tribe, Elizabeth Twining, The Natural Order of Plants, 1855

p. 25: Bay Tree - Laurus Nobilis Bay, John Sibthorp, Flora Graeca, 1823

p. 30: Le Cypres, G. De N. Regnault

p. 32: Dictamus fraxinella or dittany or gas plant, by E. Kychicus 1703 for Duchess of Beaufort

p. 77: Hawthorn or May(Ccrataegus monogyna) from The Spirit of the Woods, 1837

p. 105: The Grass Tribe, E. Twining, Kew Library

THE BRIDGEMAN ART LIBRARY

p. 15: Delphinium: Ajacis (Larkspur) c. 1568, by J.le Moyne de Morgues, (c.1530-88), Victoria & Albert Museum, London/Bridgeman Art Library, London

p. 47: Narcissus Lazetta from 'Trew Plantae Selectae' by Redoute, Pierre Joseph (1759-1804), Linnean Society, London/Bridgeman Art Library, London

p. 29: Hyacinth: "Eastern Hyacinths" (3 colours), by John Edwards, 1788 (print) Private Collection/Bridgeman Art Library, London

p. 33: Diana the Hunter by Gentileschi, Orazio (1565-1647), Musee des Beaux-Arts, Nantes/Giraudon/Bridgeman Art Library, London

p. 36: Ceres by Bianchi, Pietro (1694-1704), Christie's, London/Bridgeman Art Library, London

p. 47: Narcissus Lazetta from 'Trew Plantae Selectae' by Redoute, Pierre Joseph (1759-1804), Linnean Society, London/Bridgeman Art Library, London

p. 49: Narcissus by Rubens, Peter Paul (1577-1640), Museum Boymans-Van Beuningen, Rotterdam/Bridgeman Art Library, London

p. 55: Vertumnus and Pomona by Kessel, Jan van the Elder (1626-79), Johnny Van Haeften Gallery, London/Bridgeman Art Library, London

p. 62: Tomb painting: the departed before Osiris, Isis and Thoth, c.2850 BC, Egyptian National Museum, Cairo/Bridgeman Art Library, London

p. 69: Worcestershire Willow pattern plate (transfer printed) by Grainger Lee & Company, c.1850 Worcester, Hanley Museum & Art Gallery, Staffs/Bridgeman Art Library, London

p. 70: Flowering Apple Tree and Willow, 1991Easton, Timothy (living artist), Private Collection/Bridgeman Art Library, London

p. 8: The Beguiling of Merlin from 'Idylls of the Kind' by Alfred Tennyson (1809-92), 1870-74 by Burne-Jones Sir Edward (1833-98), Lady Lever Art Gallery, Port Sunlight/Bridgeman Art Library, London

p. 88: Mistletoe from 'A Curious Herbal', 1782 by Blackwell, Elizabeth (fl.1737), Private Collection/Bridgeman Art Library, London

p. 91: Morgan le Fay: Queen of Avalon by Sandys, Anthony Frederick Augustus (1829-1904, Birmingham City Museums & Art Gallery/Bridgeman Art Library, London

p. 103: Indian Encampment on Lake Huron by Kane, Paul (1810-71), Royal Ontario Museum, Toronto/Bridgeman Art Library, London

FINE ART PHOTOGRAPHS

Front cover & p. 6: A Tribute to Bacchus, Jean-Baptiste Robie (1821-1910)

p. 23: Apollo in the Chariot of the Sun, Bridgman, Frederik Arthur, (1847-1928), Courtesy of Galerie Berko

p. 41: A Tribute to Bacchus, Anonymous, Victoria, 19/20 Century

p. 54: Diana and Pomona, Jan Breughel, (1568-1625), Baumkotter Gallery

p. 73: Madonna and Child with St John the Baptist, Giovanni Battista Utili Da Faenza

p. 83: John the Baptist Preaching, Anonymous, (Flemish), 17th Century

p. 85: King Arthur's Wood, Elizabeth Adela Stanhope Forbes, (1859-1912)

IVY HANSEN PHOTOGRAPHY

p. 26, p. 51, p. 68

JOHN HEMPHILL

p. 13, p. 32, p. 45, p. 60, p. 74, p. 79, p. 82, p. 92

ACKNOWLEDGMENTS

BOOKS ABOUT GODS AND GODDESSES in mythological stories, read when young, remain in the memory – vivid, romantic, and real. Re-reading their legends was like renewing old friendships. Research was enhanced by the kindness of friends who spontaneously lent us special books that are now out of print. One friend's library yielded a wealth of rare and valuable material, and we are profoundly grateful for the interest shown in preparing the work. Literature held by The State Library of N.S.W., and The Woollahra Library, have been excellent sources of information.

The ancient Greek and Roman legends in this book have been researched from a number of well-established sources. Sometimes the Greek legends differ from one another according to each author's interpretation; when this happens, we seek confirmation of the most accepted version by turning to the impeccable *A Smaller Classical Dictionary* edited by E.H. Blakeney M.A. P. & O's Swan Hellenic Cruises, and their 2-week tour in M.T.S. "ORPHEUS" called "Lands of Gods and Heroes" was illuminating in every way. Two eminent guest Professors and a distinguished Canon, gave erudite lectures that were easily comprehended and enjoyed by non-academics. We appreciate the company's gift to passengers of "Cruise Handbooks 1& 11", which have been constantly referred to. Scholarly Greek guides accompanied shore excursions to sites in this unforgettably beautiful country, still vibrating with the glory of ancient Greece for those who seek it.

Our warm thanks to Deborah Nixon, Publishing Manager, Lansdowne Publishing, for her enthusiastic interest in this book from the beginning, and her sensitive approach to its production. Jenny Coren has been a supportive editor, her dedication to the work is greatly appreciated. Thanks also to Michelle Wiener for her beautiful designs.

BIBLIOGRAPHY

Anthony King, Eleanor, *Bible Plants for American Gardens,* (Dover Publications Inc., New York, 1975)

Blakeney, E.H., *A Smaller Classical Dictionary,* (M.A. J.M. Dent & Sons, London, 1927)

Briggs, Katherine, *A Dictionary of Fairies,* (Penguin Books, UK, 1977)

Bulfinch, Thomas, *Myths of Greece and Rome,* With an introduction by Joseph Campbell, (Penguin Books, USA, 1981)

Cavendish, Richard (Ed), *Legends of the World.,* (Orbis Publishing, London, 1982)

Coats, Alice M, *Flowers and Their Histories,* (Hulton Press, London, 1956)

Cox, Donovan & Jones, Hyne, *Before the Doctor Comes,* (Thorsons Publishers Ltd, UK, 1976)

Cunliffe, Barry (Ed), Cruise Handbook 1: *Landscape and People* Cruise 2: Greece and Yugoslavia Swan Hellenic Ltd, (Opus, UK, 1990)

Divine, Marguerite, *Stories from Ancient Egypt* (Burke Publishing Company Ltd., Great Britain, 1965)

Ellis, Jean A., *From the Dreamtime,* (CollinsDove., Australia, 1991)

Frazer, J.G., *The Golden Bough.* Volume 1, (McMillan & Co. Ltd., London, 1912)

Gordon, Lesley, *Green Magic ,* (A Webb and Bower Book, Ebury Press, London, 1977)

Gordon, Lesley, *The Mystery and Magic of Trees and Flowers,* (Webb and Bower, UK,1985)

Greive, M, *A Modern Herbal,* (Hafner Publishing Co., New York, 1959)

Guerber, H.A., *The Myths of Greece and Rome,* (George G. Harrap and Co., London, 1910)

Hamilton, Edith, *Mythology,* (A Mentor Book, Penguin Books, USA, 1969)

Harmsworth's Universal Encyclopedia. Volumes 1-12, (The Educational Book Co. Ltd., London, 1923)

Hemphill, John and Rosemary, *Hemphill's Book of Herbs,* (Lansdowne Publishing Pty Ltd, Sydney, 1990)

Hemphill, John and Rosemary, *The Fragrant Garden,* Angus & Robertson, Sydney, 1991)

Hepper, F. Nigel, *Pharaoh's Flowers,* (HMSO Publications Centre, London, 1990)

Jordan, Michael, *Myths of the World A Thematic Encyclopedia* (Kyle Cathie Limited, UK 1993)

Kupher, Grace H., *Legends of Greece & Rome,* (George G. Harrap & Co. Ltd, Great Britain, 1973)

Lake, Max, *Scents and Sensuality,* (Futura, London, 1993)

Lambert, Johanna (Ed), *Wise Women of the Dreamtime* (Inner Traditions International, 1993)

Malory, Sir Thomas, *Le Morte d'Arthur,* (Penguin Books, UK, 1987)

Mayhew, Ann, *The Rose,* (Mayhew Books Ltd., UK, 1979)

Mountford, Charles P., *Legends of the Dreamtime* (International Limited Editions, Australia, 1971)

Oldham, John and Ray, *Gardens in Time,* (Lansdowne Press, Sydney, 1980)

Parker, Derek & Julie, *The Immortals, The mysterious world of Gods, Goblins, Fairies, Leprechauns, Vampires, Witches and Devils,* (Webb & Bower, Great Britain, 1976)

Powell, Claire, *The Meaning of Flowers,* Jupiter Books, London, 1977)

Ratsch, Christian, *The Dictionary of Sacred and Magical Plants,* (ABC-Clio, 1992)

Reed, A.W., *Aboriginal Legends,* (Reed Books Pty Ltd, Australia 1987)

Renault, Mary, *The King Must Die,* (Longmans, Green & Co., London, 1958) Rogers, Jo (Ed), *What Food is That?* (Lansdowne Publishing Pty Ltd, Sydney, 1990)

Sanecki, Kay N., *The Complete Book of Herbs,* (Macdonald and Jane's: London, 1975)

Sfikas, George, *Medicinal Plants of Greece,* (Efstathiadis Group S.A., 1993)

Spence, Lewis, *Egypt,* (Studio Editions, London, 1990)

Stirling Macoboy, *What Flower is That?,* (Lansdowne Publishing Pty Ltd, Sydney, 1974)

Stuart, Malcolm (Ed), *The Encyclopedia of Herbs and Herbalism* (Books for Pleasure, Sydney, 1979)

Tredennick, Hugh and Tarrant, Harold, T*he Last Days of Socrates,* Plato, (Penguin Books, London, 1993)

Watterson, Barbara, *The Gods of Ancient Egypt,* (B.T. Batsford Ltd., London, 1984)

Wilson, Barbara Ker, *The Willow Pattern Story* (Angus and Robertson Publishers, Australia, 1978)

Zimmer Bradley, Marion, *The Mists of Avalon,* (A Del Ray Book, Ballantine Books, New York, 1982)

INDEX